The Art of
FAST
PLAY

The Art of
FAST
PLAY

Solving Golf's
Maddening Problem
of Slow Play

By Sam Dunn

Illustrations By Melissa Detroy

VINEYARD STORIES
Edgartown, Massachusetts

Published by Vineyard Stories
52 Bold Meadow Road
Edgartown, MA 02539
508 221 2338
www.vineyardstories.com

Library of Congress Control Number: 2012956125
ISBN: 978-0-9849136-2-6

Book Design: Jill Dible, Atlanta, GA

Printed in China

"Play Hard, Play Fair, Play Fast!"

SIGN AT THE FIRST TEE OF A CALIFORNIA GOLF COURSE

Note on Gender

Every writer faces a dilemma. When writing about people (or in this case, golfers) the writer usually means both men and women. That is certainly true in this book. The dilemma is whether every time the writer is referring to a golfer is it really necessary to say "he or she" did this or that? A more awkward and stilted phrase hasn't been conceived.

So my apologies in advance for sticking to the old school and using the masculine.

No slight is intended.

Contents

INTRODUCTION

"When I hear people complain about slow play, I think about what Mark Twain said about the weather: Everybody talks about it but nobody does anything about it."

— PETER KOSTIS

IT WAS A STUNNING MOMENT when Rory McIlroy won the 2011 U.S. Open. He was only 22 years old, and he destroyed the opposition. But perhaps the most remarkable thing was that, in an age when pro and recreational golfers alike are taking five hours to play a round of golf, he was stepping up to the ball and striking it—beautifully, it goes without saying—mere seconds after it was his turn to hit. Had he been in a foursome of like-minded players he could have finished his rounds in well under four hours. To my way of thinking he showed us how the game is supposed to be played. But more to the point he showed that *pace of play is unrelated to performance.*

I conclude this despite having no particular golf expertise. I don't consider myself a great player, or even a very good one. I'm an architect (a building architect, not a golf course architect). I once designed a clubhouse, and I was once involved in developing a golf course. But I do not earn my living in the golf business. Nothing qualifies me to write about golf except that I truly love the game. It's been important to me in many ways—as an absorbing pastime; as a continuing source of pleasure and a bonding experience with friends; as a rich, interesting travel template; and as a pursuit that bonds me closely to my children, two of whom seem to be following me lockstep into a lifelong love affair with golf.

As do many who love the game, a visceral pleasure courses through my bones when I strike a shot squarely. I feel a sense of exhilaration in watching my ball soar against the sky, and a joy in watching a shot or a long putt actually disappear into the impossibly small target of a four-inch hole. I can't wait to get on the course. I love this game.

People tell me I have a type-A personality, and I guess I'd agree that I'm pretty impatient. But golf relaxes me. I get lost in the challenge and the experience—until, that is, I run into the brick wall of slow play. It gets me seething, it puts me at wits' end. It destroys the pleasure of the game I love. I want to wring somebody's neck, but I don't even know who's responsible. How and why is this happening to our beloved game? Bobby Jones and Gene Sarazen didn't complain about slow play, but today everybody does.

It seems obvious that at private clubs a culture of fast play takes hold naturally. Everyone knows the course in detail, there are caddies to help out, and most of the golfers are frequent players. Kids learn from their parents. And there is considerable peer pressure; the rare slow players become pariahs if they don't change.

There was a time when golf was not widely available outside of private clubs, but that is changing rapidly. There's an emerging new landscape in public golf. In recent decades, all over the world, the daily-fee course has become ubiquitous. More difficult and far more interesting than the traditional muni, the daily-fee course holds many of the characteristics of the private club, but without the self-regulating culture of fast play. Kids don't learn from their parents out here. People learn on the fly. There's very little peer pressure because most golfers on a course at any given moment are strangers.

This surge in daily-fee construction has some 25 million souls in America alone calling themselves golfers. This number includes millions of new converts. It has succeeded in removing the long-attached stigma that only rich old men in country clubs have access to golf. But in the midst of this growth and enthusiasm, a widening crisis in public golf is at hand: *It is taking so long to play a round of golf that the game is in danger of being ruined.*

In public golf the four-hour round is all but extinct. Any round under four and a half hours is practically a sprint. This book is called *The Art of Fast Play* since most golfers now seem to expect five-hour rounds. I've played my share of slow rounds, and I find it hard to believe that five hours is a normal pace for anyone. I know that my foursome tends to fall apart when the pace slows to a crawl. Tempers fray, shots go wild, and clubs get slammed into the ground.

With the aid of instruction and their own devotion to golf, many new players have honed a decent game. But many are clueless about how to play at a reasonable pace. It's not just new golfers. Many lifelong devotees have never figured it out. Some players eventually get the hang of it. Many don't. It is astonishing to see the things we do on the course—leaving bags and carts in front of the green, standing around while someone on the other side of the fairway is looking for a ball, walking hundreds of feet to retrieve a rake that got passed on the way into a trap, hitting do-overs on the course, going repeatedly through a vexing preshot routine, standing idle on the green because no one knows who's away, and on and on and on.

It is a fact that the golfing community at large has never been taught how to play at a proper pace. Hundreds of books and publications are devoted to the subject of teaching the game of golf. Thousands of PGA professionals at local courses and at dozens of specialized golf schools around the country are similarly focused. But among the myriad opportunities to learn the game, one is hard-pressed to find more than a passing reference to anything having to do with pace of play. I suppose this is understandable because it isn't a very glamorous subject. A swing coach can become a celebrity, but who wants to be known as the great theorist of bag management or cart placement?

Many have become resigned to the status quo. They accept the five-and-a-half-hour round as a given. I haven't been able to do this. It doesn't suit my personality, and besides, even though I'm no golf expert I know in my bones it doesn't have to be this way. And I love this game too much to stand idly by and let it be compromised by something that doesn't have to be. Maybe it's tilting at windmills, but I decided to try and do something about it by writing this book.

I realized that my association with golf had taken place in the perfect laboratory to understand slow play. I didn't learn the game as a child, wasn't taught by my parents, and don't belong to a country club. I'm your typical public golfer operating in the trenches. I play munis, daily-fees, resort courses—the whole gamut of public golf. I learned the golf swing and the etiquette of the game through trial and error. At one time I was part of the problem—a clueless, slow player—and no wonder. I took lessons from time to time and played all over, but *I can honestly say that no one in the golf industry ever said a word to me about how to play at a proper pace.*

So in that respect this book has been years in the making. Not in the writing, but in the experience garnered over many years of playing golf and thinking and observing. It took that long to come to the point where I felt I truly understood the mechanics of fast play.

I'm convinced that playing golf at a proper pace is a skill that can be learned. Unlike the golf swing, anyone can master it. Fast play results from certain simple procedures; it has little to do with being able to hit the ball long and straight. There is no reason why every golfer, regardless of handicap, armed with the simple strategies contained in this book, cannot learn to play a round of golf in four hours or less.

And without hurrying, I might add. Playing at a four-hour pace doesn't result from rushing around. It comes instead from simply not wasting time. There is no single big thing that will solve the problem, no miracle cure. It's about a multitude of little things. The opportunities for wasting time are many, and each is so small as to be nearly invisible. But they add up. An efficient, four-hour round will result from recognizing these wasted moments and acting to prevent them. That is the essential thesis of this book.

I don't blame anyone in particular for slow play, and I don't believe, with our golf courses as congested as they are, that any one individual can solve the problem. Readers of this book can only become faster players if the group ahead of them moves quickly enough, and the group ahead of them, and the group ahead of them. We are all in this together. The course operators and greenskeepers are in it, too, and everybody else who can make a contribution to solving a problem that threatens to destroy the sport.

Slow play looms as golf's biggest problem. The golfing community needs to master the art of fast play with all the zeal it brings to good ball striking. So allow yourself a brief detour into those prosaic subjects of bag management, cart placement, and the like. And when you are on the course, hold in your mind the image of young Rory McIlroy striding up to his ball and striking it with joy and confidence and, best of all, with no delay.

February 2013

CHAPTER 1

Keep Up the Pace

*"A typical round of golf can be played in
four hours or less with no rushing."*
—Tom Watson

IMAGINE A SOFTBALL GAME with a pitcher who is never ready, who delays every pitch because he puffs on his cigar, strolls to home plate to talk to the catcher, adjusts his glove, talks on his cell phone, has to be reminded of the count, forgets the number of outs, and wants to stop the game to tell everyone a joke. The other seventeen players would be seething. But if similar behavior takes place on the wide-open spaces of a golf course, all the other players on the course can't see it. There might be more than a hundred golfers who are being held up by the slow player, and they're seething, all right—but they probably don't even know who the person is.

Keeping up the pace is a theme heard over and over in public golf. It's a simple concept, but if the crisis of slow play tells us anything, it's that keeping up the pace is not that easy. There is a slow play demon lurking out there that haunts the golfing community. This demon never sleeps and is totally unforgiving, pouncing on every time-wasting mistake, no matter how small. His goal is to destroy the pace of play at each and every golf course each and every day. And he will—if you let him.

A Golf Course Is Like a One-Lane Bridge

Keeping the pace is essential for one reason only: A golf course is like a one-lane bridge. It really isn't possible to pass. Sure, a twosome can play through a foursome on an uncrowded course, but on a day when play is

A golf course is like a one-lane bridge.
No one can pass, and no one can go any faster than the leading car.

continuous, playing through is not an option. It will ease the frustration of the one lucky foursome that gets through, but everyone who follows will be delayed even further. The instruction "Let Faster Players Play Through" that is seen on so many scorecards should be stricken from public golf. Instead scorecards should read, "Keep Up with the Group Ahead, No Matter What." We who occupy public courses on a crowded Sunday are stuck with each other. All must cooperate in setting a suitable pace of play, or the system, which is only as strong as its weakest link, breaks down. A bumbling performance by one foursome can ruin the experience for all.

What Does "Keeping Up" Mean?

We have all heard the members of a dawdling foursome rationalize their performance with vague references to "moving as fast as possible" and "not really holding anyone up." This doesn't need to be subjective, however, as there are three simple and irrefutable tests of whether a foursome is keeping up:

- Has a group arrived at the tee as soon as the foursome ahead is hitting the last of their approach shots, if not before?
- Has it arrived at their approach shots as soon as the group ahead is walking off the green, if not before?

- If there is no one ahead of them, is the group playing fast enough so that the foursome behind is not waiting at all, except briefly at par-3s?

Gaps Are the Building Blocks of Slow Play

If a group does not meet all three of the keeping-up tests, it is too slow and has allowed a gap to develop. Gaps, as they accumulate, are the building blocks of the five-hour round. To maintain a four-hour pace it should take about 14 minutes to play a par-4. If a group falls one hole behind, the consequences are far-reaching: That group has imposed a 14-minute delay on *every group to follow for the entire day.* Add a few more gaps like this, and a five-hour round is in the making.

A Simple Notion: Making Others Wait Is Inconsiderate

Playing fast should be seen as the considerate thing to do for the many others with whom you're on the course. A golf course is a *shared space—* shared with the other members of your foursome, and shared with other foursomes. As individuals we each have a responsibility to keep up with the others in the foursome, and as a foursome we have a responsibility to keep up with the foursome in front of ours.

The fact is that, on a crowded course, slow play has a ripple effect that will inconvenience every golfer who follows for the rest of the day.

Keeping up—individually within a group and as a foursome in front of other groups—must be done at all costs. This book will make it easier and more enjoyable to do this. Usually this will mean paying more attention and doing things better, but sometimes it may mean picking up if we are holding up our foursome, or even that our whole foursome might forgo putting and just move to the next tee. In extreme cases it may mean a more draconian action, such as skipping an entire hole. *In short, making others wait unnecessarily must become behavior that we will not permit in ourselves or our foursome.*

A Slow Round Is Made in Tiny Increments

Fast play isn't accomplished by hurrying. It's accomplished by a far easier, more relaxing, and simpler idea. *Fast play is accomplished by simply not wasting time.* It's vital to understand that slow rounds are a result of an accumulation of tiny misdemeanors.

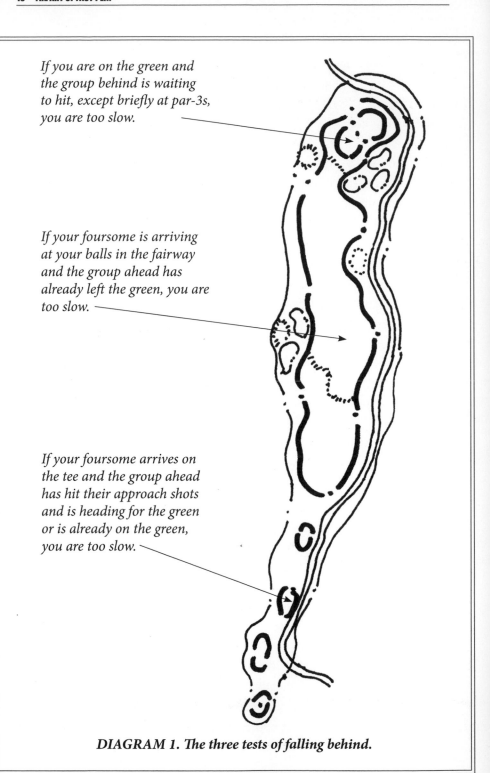

If you are on the green and the group behind is waiting to hit, except briefly at par-3s, you are too slow.

If your foursome is arriving at your balls in the fairway and the group ahead has already left the green, you are too slow.

If your foursome arrives on the tee and the group ahead has hit their approach shots and is heading for the green or is already on the green, you are too slow.

DIAGRAM 1. *The three tests of falling behind.*

As a famous architect once said, "God is in the details." This is undeniably true of the golf swing, indeed of any task well done. So, too, it is with playing faster.

The opportunities for wasting time on the golf course are numerous beyond counting, and each one is measured in mere seconds. This book could be titled "Ten Wasted Seconds Will Ruin Your Round," because it is literally increments of only 10 seconds or so of wasted time that accumulate to make a five-hour round. This tiny, almost invisible, amount of time is at stake at every moment during a round, and the accumulation of these moments is relentless and irreversible. Seconds become minutes. Minutes become an hour, or even two.

I cannot emphasize this enough. If the attitude is "It will only waste a minute to do this thing or that thing," the point will have been missed. Once a group lets down its guard, these minor transgressions will multiply and spread like a virus.

To illustrate, here are a few examples of the multitude of small ways players can waste time on the course:

- After hitting an approach shot, does a golfer get in the cart straightaway and drive off so those behind can hit, or does he stand behind the cart and wipe down his club, put on the head cover, and stow it before getting in and driving away?
- When parking at the green, does a golfer put the cart behind the putting surface so when the foursome walks off the green, the group behind can hit, or is he content to park beside the green, meaning the next foursome can't hit until he and his partners have put their clubs away and driven off?
- How long does the golfer actually take to hit a shot? As we will see later, we have only 20 seconds to hit. If a golfer takes 30 seconds, it will add 10 seconds for every shot taken, which really adds up over the course of a round.
- Does the golfer enter a bunker close to the ball or walk all over the bunker, leaving a long line of footprints to rake?
- When on the tee with an open fairway ahead, does the golfer choose that time to tell a new joke, or does he wait for a better time?

- Does the golfer find himself ready to tee off, only to remember he broke his tee on the previous hole, meaning his playing partners stand idle while he tries to locate one somewhere in the bowels of his bag?

I could easily cite many more examples, but you get the picture.

Situational Awareness

Not wasting time is the key, and that sounds simple enough. But without a true sense of awareness on the course it won't happen. Being alert and aware is a state of mind. It means keeping our antenna out and tuned so we absorb our surroundings and compute what needs to be done. It means keeping our heads up and our eyes open, taking in and processing the situation around us, and being ready to do our part to ensure a proper pace for our foursome. We might call this *situational awareness.*

Not to overstate the point, but without a good degree of situational awareness all is lost in this battle against slow play. You can't keep up if you don't even know you're behind.

We aren't all necessarily born with a gift of situational awareness, much as we might not have been given a natural sense of rhythm or a keen sense of taste. So if we are among the unlucky ones who don't have situational awareness, we need to nurture and develop it. All of us in the golfing fraternity must learn to keep the notion of staying alert and aware near the front of our consciousness when we are on the course. How we do it really isn't important, but do it we must.

For me, after I've hit a shot I ask myself what, if anything, I am obligated to do at that moment to keep a good pace. Do I need to get out of the way quickly so that someone else in my group can hit? Do I need to get in the cart and clear the landing zone so that the group behind can hit? Do I need to grab some clubs and hustle off to a shot I've just blasted into the woods? Do I need to mark my ball? Do I need to tend the flag for someone else?

Similarly, each time someone else in my foursome hits a shot I ask myself what, if anything, I can do at that moment to help our foursome keep a good pace. If someone's shot is heading for the woods I try to watch it carefully because I might be the only one who sees where it comes to rest. If someone in my foursome takes a big divot and I am nearby, I'll toss it back. If someone else is widely separated from the cart, I offer to drive it. If someone has walked up to the green and I am in the cart, I will remember to bring his putter.

It's not like I'm focused on these things at the exclusion of all else. In fact, at this point I do it almost subconsciously. Like so many things we do in life—shifting gears in the car, tying our shoes—it has become second nature. We talk about building a repeating swing, making it automatic. This habit of awareness can be thought of in the same way. We need to groove our sense of awareness much as we hope to groove our golf swing. The good news is, it's a whole lot easier.

Be a Team Player

Playing fast takes a team effort. We need to be ready to help our companions and they us.

It is not an exaggeration to say that if a foursome is to play at a proper pace, everyone needs, on every single hole, to take some action above and beyond just playing their own ball. Will we be alert enough to notice these things and act on them?

Here are a few of the hundreds of scenarios I could cite:

- Let's say a player is not away, but the golfer who is needs some time to assess his shot because his ball is behind a tree. Will the player who is closer to the green notice this and hit first to keep things moving? Or will he not pick up on it and allow his group to waste the time that could be saved if he took the initiative to hit first?
- Will a golfer happen to notice that his partner is in a bunker but there are no rakes nearby? If he does, he could toss his partner one, so that he doesn't have to go looking for one while everyone else is waiting.
- After a golfer has hit his drive in the fairway, does he watch the slice his partner hits into the woods, giving him a second set of eyes to locate his ball? Or does he turn away to stow his driver because it really isn't his problem?
- Will a golfer notice that his partner left a club next to the green? If not, his foursome could find itself waiting a long time while his partner drives around the course looking for it after he finally realizes that it's missing.

- On a hole where carts are confined to the paths, will the golfer pick up on the fact that both of his opponents are on the opposite side of the fairway from their cart and offer to drive it to the green for them? Or will he be oblivious and climb into his cart with his partner and drive away, only to have to wait for them at the green while they walk all the way across the course to retrieve their cart?
- If a golfer's partner has been driving the cart all day and he has been content to leave his partner with the responsibility, will he notice when his partner hits a shot short and wide of the green on the side opposite the path and take over the driving duties for the remainder of the hole? Or will he assume it's business as usual and leave him with the awkward and time-consuming job of parking the cart on one side of the course and playing his shot from the other?

It's only natural to be mostly concerned about our own games and our own scores, and we can't be expected to pay the same kind of attention to others. Having said that, there's a happy medium. We don't want to be like the self-absorbed golfer we have all played with at some point. You know: the one who's in his own world, who never remembers to bring a putter to his partner, who never tends the flag and doesn't help look for lost balls. Who doesn't even notice the birdie you just made. Who will never be the one to say to his foursome, "The group behind is waiting, we need to get moving." In short he doesn't see and compute his surroundings beyond what he needs to do to play his own ball, and he doesn't do even that with an eye to being efficient. This is the polar opposite of being alert and aware. *It's incompatible with fast play because it takes an unselfish eye and a cooperative mentality to play fast.*

Here's a good and simple test for yourself and others: If, after completion of a hole, a golfer does not know the scores made by the others in the foursome, then that golfer is not sufficiently aware and alert to contribute to the team effort required to play fast. This does not mean on every hole and in every situation every golfer needs to know what every other golfer did or he's a self-absorbed you-know-what. But if he never seems to know anybody's score, he isn't paying attention and probably doesn't care. He's not going to be a considerate, helpful member of the foursome. In short, he's not a team player.

One More Time: Slow Rounds Are Made from Tiny Mistakes

I suspect many of you aren't ready to accept that each and every small delay is all that meaningful in the big scheme of things. My playing companions used to look at me like I was crazy when I would point out some minor thing we could have done better. They would say something like, "You've gotta be kidding me. Taking an extra 30 seconds to write down these scores can't possibly make any difference. Get a life, will ya?"

But slowly, as the weight of the sheer number of chances to waste time in a round of golf began to sink in, they bought into the idea.

It's truly relentless, this demon of slow play, and it never rests. It's there on every single hole, indeed on every single shot, and it will break you if you let it. So if you do nothing else about fast play, get on this bandwagon to be alert to every opportunity to save time, no matter how small.

SUMMARY: Keep Up the Pace

- A golf course is like a one-lane bridge. It isn't possible to pass, so the only alternative is to keep up the pace. When play is continuous, playing through is not an option.
- A group is too slow if it is not directly behind the group in front.
- If there is no one in front of them, a group is too slow if the group behind is waiting at all, except briefly at the par-3s.
- A group must keep up at all costs, even if this means picking up or skipping a hole.
- Making others wait on the golf course is inconsiderate, intolerable behavior that a player should not permit personally or in the foursome.
- Slow play has a ripple effect, inconveniencing every golfer who follows for the rest of the day.
- Slow rounds are made up of tiny increments of wasted time.
- Situational awareness is the key to recognizing moments of wasted time and acting to avoid them.
- A team player helps others in the foursome keep a proper pace.
- A good test of awareness is whether a golfer generally knows the scores of the rest of the foursome at the completion of a hole.

CHAPTER 2

Find It and Hit It

"You can play bad, but you can't play slow."
—Charles Barkley

EVERYONE ON THE GOLF COURSE, regardless of the number of shots they are taking, must move at the same pace. Both beginners and high-handicappers, because they are taking more shots than better or more experienced players, need to move faster and hit sooner.

Can Beginners and High-Handicappers Be Expected to Keep Up?

Recently at a semiprivate course my son and I were paired with two men we had never met. After observing their practice swings on the first tee, we were certain that it would be a long day. One was not an experienced player, but he was a touring pro compared to Joe. Joe had the most atrocious golf swing possible, a loopy spaghetti-like backswing that, in a flash, became a reckless, gyrating downswing delivered with all his might. He was a real Charles Barkley. My son and I looked at each other. There was no way this swing could produce anything that resembled a reasonable golf shot.

He addressed the ball on the first tee and promptly whiffed, nearly falling over. We have all witnessed a whiff. More often than not the perpetrator acts totally nonchalant, as though it was just another practice swing. But Joe looked up at us, displayed a wry smile, and put his forefinger to his lips, as if to say, "It's our secret. Don't tell anyone." I thought, *I could get to like this guy*. He then hit an astonishing smother hook that I swear had the ball going 90 degrees dead left when it entered the woods. "Mulligan, Joe?" I suggested. "No, man, that was one of my better shots."

We started down the fairway. "They seem nice," I said to my son, putting the best spin I could think of on the situation. He wasn't buying it. "Yeah, but Joe's gonna shoot 150 and it'll take us six hours to play. Let's go help him find his ball." But when we looked over toward Joe, we noticed that he was far ahead of us, walking strongly and purposefully toward the woods. He seemed to know exactly where he was going. He had looked intently at the flight of his tee shot, I remembered. And before we could even get to the woods to help him, his ball came flying out. He had found it and chipped out. Even so the ball was still far short of our drives, but he walked directly to it and hit it again before we could even catch up to him. It took him three more to reach the green, including a brief visit to the woods on the opposite side of the fairway. His first putt went far by the whole, and his comebacker was far short. "Eight is enough," he said cheerfully (ignoring the whiff), and picked up.

This proved to be a harbinger of the round. Joe hit a remarkable collection of bad golf shots, but was determined to keep up with the foursome. He watched his errant shots and walked directly to them. If we couldn't find his ball in a minute or so, he pulled another from his well-stocked collection and moved on. He didn't hit do-overs, he didn't hit provisional balls, he moved steadily ahead with little wasted motion. And he displayed nothing but good humor throughout. In response to some of his more erratic shots we named him "The Trick Shot Artist," and he was delighted by this.

We got to know him as the round progressed. He had recently taken up the game, and while he had had little success to date he had fallen in love with golf. He had recently made his first par and was still glowing from the experience. He was trying his best and, sure enough, before the round was over it paid off. He produced a few good shots toward the end, and on the short par-3 17th, he made the second par of his life.

On reflection, it was an amazing performance. He had probably taken every one of the 150 shots that my son had predicted, but we never once felt burdened by his utter lack of experience or his inability to hit more than a few serviceable golf shots. We never had to wait.

He hadn't mastered the game of golf, but he had mastered the Art of Finding it And Hitting It. He had mastered the Art of Picking Up.

Often a foursome is burdened by a bad or beginning player. Playing partners become hostage to lost balls, provisional shots, do-overs, "floating" mulligans, unwillingness to pick up, and often bad humor and anger. The high-maintenance high-handicapper is the one without a game yet he steals the show. Joe showed us a better way: It doesn't matter if you are a rank beginner or just a bad player: If you will commit it to two simple principles—*find it and hit it and pick up after eight shots*—you can play with anybody.

Experienced Players: You Are Not Immune to Slow Play

A few weeks after the round with Joe, my regular Saturday foursome was short one player, and we were joined by a friend of a friend. He was a good player on the verge of breaking 80. But by the third hole we were tearing our hair out. He was deliberate by nature, but this was not the only problem. It was what he did between shots that put us over the edge—which was . . . nothing at all. He would sit glassy-eyed in the cart until it was his turn to hit, then begin an agonizing process of club selection and shot planning. After enduring this preshot routine, we prayed that an insect would not select this moment to land on his ball as it had on the second hole. When this happened he insisted on stepping away and starting the whole tortuous process again. When he wasn't dawdling over his ball he seemed in a daze. He left his clubs lying around. He had no idea who was away. In short, this experienced player conducted himself as though he lived in a vacuum. He did not recognize that he was in a shared space.

Playing Fast versus Playing Well

Although many good players are also fast (to wit, Rory McIlroy), playing well does not necessarily equate to playing fast. Touring pros, even though they have caddies and forecaddies, are notoriously slow:

- Time for a pro twosome to play a round   4 hours
- Time for a pro threesome to play a round   5 hours
- Time for a pro foursome to play a round   N/A

Professional tournaments don't play foursomes for obvious reasons. In the occasional pro-am event played in foursomes, a round can take six hours.

It is easy to be seduced by the notion that fewer strokes automatically mean less time. For you good players out there, it's worth remembering this and taking a look in the mirror from time to time.

SUMMARY: Find It and Hit It

⚲ Beginners and high-handicappers must commit to finding their ball and hitting it with dispatch. They will have to move faster and hit sooner than their playing partners.

⚲ They should pick up after eight shots per hole.

⚲ Experienced players should not automatically assume that they are playing fast enough. Playing well does not necessarily mean playing fast.

CHAPTER 3

When It's Your Turn, Be Ready to Hit

"You know it's a joke when you're stuck with a slowpoke,
I'm wearin' a frown 'cause I'm paired with this clown,
We don't like, We don't like, We don't like slow play!"
—THE PGA TOUR BAND, JAKE TROUT AND THE FLOUNDERS
(PETER JACOBSON, MARK LYE, THE LATE PAYNE STEWART, AND LARRY RINKER)

ALTHOUGH THERE ARE EXCEPTIONS, generally only one member of a foursome can hit at any given moment. *A fast pace will be established in large measure by reducing the down time between shots.* Accordingly, it's fundamental for each of us to be ready to hit our shot when our turn comes up.

Ten Wasted Seconds Will Ruin Your Round

It goes without saying that golf is far more pleasurable when played at a proper pace. This is just as true on an empty course as on one packed to the gills. When all is right with the pace of play and the chemistry within the foursome, the game is free-flowing and pleasurable in the extreme. There is time enough to take the game seriously, study one's shots, and prepare to hit them. There is no sense of urgency. At the same time there is little down time beyond observing the shots of the other players in the foursome, which, for the real golfer, is in itself a pleasure and a learning experience. The group operates as a team. Each player is aware of the others and their positions on the course. They hit in sequence with little wasted time. They help each other when necessary—looking for lost balls, tending the flag, tossing a rake, bringing a putter to a partner, and so forth. There is ample time between shots to drink in the scenery, watch the wildlife on the course, chat with the others in the foursome. When done right it is an efficient, yet relaxed experience that reaches another level.

But consider this: If the players in the foursome are taking, say, an extra 10 seconds—only 10 seconds—to hit each of their shots, this pleasurable experience is transformed. A full hour is added to the round, an hour of dead time and the consequent annoyance and boredom for not only the members of the foursome but the groups behind. Ten seconds! Don't believe it? Do the math.

If each player shoots 90, that's a total for the foursome of 360 shots. If each shot takes an extra 10 seconds, that's 3,600 seconds—which comes to one hour. *A four-hour round just became five.*

Wasting only 10 seconds per shot adds an hour to the round.

The startling truth is that wasting time in increments of only 10 seconds per shot can add a full hour to the round. This addresses only the actual execution of the shots. As we all know there are a multitude of other possibilities for wasting time. An hour can become an hour and a half or even two.

The tyranny of these transgressions, each of which seems so insignificant, is that cumulatively they will destroy the pleasure of a round of golf.

Be Realistic: It Takes Time to Play a Round of Golf

A proper round of golf for a foursome will take close to four hours. Anyone who claims less doesn't care enough about the game to take it seriously. The average golf course these days is 7,000 yards long. Even though most of us don't play at this length we will walk more than the full length of the course, considering the distance between greens and tees. In total we will walk more than four miles if we stay right on the centerlines of the holes. It's a nice thought, but the reality is that we will visit a number of remote regions of the course during the round. It is likely that we will walk a total of five miles or more. At a good walking speed of about three and a half miles per hour it will take a good hour and a half just to cover the distance required to play the round of golf.

Carts Aren't That Fast

Riding in carts doesn't significantly reduce this time, because even though carts cover ground in a big hurry, they actually slow things down around the greens and in rough terrain. The next time you are in a foursome when two of the players are walking and two riding, take note of whether the walkers are actually slowing things up.

You will discover that if all four players are in the fairway, yes, it will certainly take the walkers longer to get to their balls, but they will generally be ready to hit their second shots by the time the riders have hit theirs. (And hit they should, regardless of who's away. More on this later.) If the players are not in the fairway—the more likely outcome—the riders won't have much advantage because carts can't go driving around in steep terrain, woods, or desert, or on mounds or green complexes. The occupants will have to get out and walk to their balls, and remember: the cart is serving two golfers who could easily have deposited their drives on opposite sides of the fairway. For all its capabilities, a golf cart cannot be in two places at once.

Following their second shots, the walkers will likely arrive at the green sooner than the riders because of all the jostling and repositioning of carts that is required around the green.

The experience at Bandon Dunes, the Oregon golf resort, is telling. One would imagine this oceanside complex of four courses would experience slow golf in the extreme because of the difficult conditions—wind and lots of it, wild grasses, gorse, titanic dunes, giant waste areas, and heavy bunkering, not to mention the distraction of some of the most amazing vistas to be found anywhere in the game. Yet golf here is played in four hours as a matter of course. Why am I telling you this? Because *Bandon Dunes is a walking-only facility.* When a foursome walks, everyone is proceeding directly to their balls with all of their equipment all of the time. There is no wasted motion, and this more than makes up for any lack of speed.

Anatomy of a Four-Hour Round

So it isn't a foregone conclusion that carts are going to be faster. They are definitely slower if they are not permitted to leave the paths. The 90-minute travel time required for a round holds whether a group is riding or walking.

This leaves, on average, two and a half hours—150 minutes—to locate balls and to plan and play the shots. Based on a typical foursome's total of 360 shots (an average of 90 per player), 25 seconds per shot is available. After subtracting a five-second-per-shot safety factor for unavoidable delays such as looking for lost balls—a total of 30 minutes—you have about 20 seconds to hit each shot. This is an average. Tee shots may take longer since the teeing ground is shared. On the other hand, tap-ins take almost no time.

To review how we use the time in an average four-hour round:

- Travel time, including green to tee = 90 minutes
- Unavoidable delays such as looking for lost balls, stopping at the turn, going to the bathroom, replacing divots, general housekeeping = 30 minutes

- Preparation and execution of shots (360 shots @ 20 seconds each) = 120 minutes

TOTAL = 240 minutes (four hours)

The key number is the 20 seconds to hit each shot. It might not sound like enough time to plan and hit a shot, but *it's plenty of time if players are ready to hit when it is their turn.* All the preparations for most shots can usually be accomplished while others are hitting. On the other hand, if a player is not ready to hit, 20 seconds will clearly not be enough time. If this time leaks by only 10 seconds, a miserable experience is in the making for your group and all who follow.

It's important to note that 20 seconds is the *maximum* time you have. The equation is based on shooting 90, which most golfers can't do. A player who is going to take 100 shots obviously needs to hit each shot a little quicker.

Players have approximately 20 seconds to hit each shot in a four-hour round.

It's interesting to note that the PGA Tour has a policy on this. It allows a player 45 seconds to hit a shot. Taking longer can mean a penalty for slow play. We all know that professionals are involved in serious business and would expect them to take longer to hit a shot than the average player. This goes a long way to explaining why threesomes of Tour players need five hours to play a round. But it also tells us if we emulate the pros (who, remember, are hitting many fewer shots than we are) what we are in for. Recreational players cannot even think about taking 45 seconds to play a shot if the goal is four-hour golf. We have 20 seconds, no more.

Distractions on the Tee

Obviously each hole begins with a tee shot. The situation is ideal for a quick and efficient getaway. The whereabouts of all the players and their balls are known, and there should be a minimum of contemplation over club selection as the exact distance to the hole is easily deduced and the stance and lie are perfect. Yet we have all seen foursomes standing on the tee doing nothing. Why?

These golfers are standing around on the tee. Someone should be hitting.

- The player who has the honor doesn't realize it.
- The player with the honor is doing something else: recording scores from the last hole, getting a drink of water, looking for a tee, putting on sun block.
- Someone has picked this moment to tell a joke heard the night before. Sure, the occasion of playing golf is enhanced by tall tales and jokes—and earnest talk, too—but if the fairway is clear, golf is the first order of business.
- No one else in the foursome has taken the initiative to hit.

Preparation for Tee Shots

It is everyone's responsibility to know the order of play on the tee. This should come naturally to anyone who was paying attention during the previous hole—which goes again to the point of being alert and aware. The player with the honor should prepare to hit straightaway. If the course is unfamiliar, the golfer can glance at the scorecard to get a general sense of the type of hole that is coming up and, while approaching the tee, peruse the hole diagram if there is one. If there's any housekeeping to do, such as cleaning clubs or writing down scores, this is not the moment. After hitting the tee shot, there's plenty of time to do these things.

Players who do not have the honor can prepare while others are hitting. If they are not leading off, there is little excuse for not having selected a club or having a concept for their shot when their turn arrives. True, occasionally something can be learned from watching another player hit that will cause a change in club selection. This is a valid reason for going back to the bag, but little else is.

When players in the same group are hitting from different tees, those hitting from the shorter tees should go directly to them to unless they are in the line of the rear tees. The obvious reason for doing this is to be prepared to hit when their turn comes. And in many instances, because they are by definition shorter hitters, they will be able to hit first. So waiting to go to their tee can be a waste of time on two counts.

Watch the Ball Intently

In order to hit a second shot, a player needs to find the first one. This job begins on the tee. When shots are in the air, it is crucially important to watch the ball intently. We all like to admire our good shots, but it is far more important to watch our bad ones. When we have hit a bad shot there is a tendency to look away in disgust. This must be resisted, as *nothing will slow a round of golf like looking for lost balls in the wrong place*. It requires a conscious and disciplined effort to watch the ball and to note some landmark like a particular tree or a rock near the line of the shot. It is amazing how different the landscape will look after arriving in the vicinity of the ball, and without a landmark a player won't have a clue where to start looking.

Watch All Shots, not Just Your Own

It is the responsibility of all members of the group to watch the shots of their playing partners. Once again we've got to be alert and aware! Four pairs of eyes increase the chances of a quick find of an errant shot by fourfold. These odds should be appealing to the entire foursome because a lost

All members of a group should try to watch the flight of every shot.

ball delays everyone, not just the player who hits it. On the tee, especially, there is no excuse for not watching every shot. We have all experienced the value of extra eyes. A shot hit into woods will often ricochet so suddenly that three players can't follow it, but the fourth will happen to see it. If not, a ball can rocket out of the woods into the fairway and go unnoticed—except by a lucky golfer from a following group who is pleased to take ownership of your brand-new Titleist.

Big quantities of time and frustration can be saved by simply watching the ball intently while it is in the air.

Listen for the Sound of Impact

It is also important to listen. It is surprising what can be learned. The particular character of the sound of impact, however faint, can help to deduce a ball's final resting place. Did you hear a "tick" of the ball hitting the cart path, indicating that it has taken a leap ahead? A "thwack" of solid contact against a tree, indicating that it has been stopped in its tracks? Multiple "thwacks"? A muffled rustling of the ball hitting leaves? Or no sound at all, indicating that the ball got through clean? These sounds can definitely help you find your ball.

Because the sound is coming from some distance away it can be barely audible and, due to the relatively slow speed of sound, a bit delayed. For this reason it is important that the foursome be quiet during the time of impact. No talking. No rustling in golf bags. Being silent for a moment is a small price to pay for possibly not having to spend the next minutes looking for someone's ball. Once the ball has come to rest you are free to berate it, or the person who hit it, at will.

The importance of this struck home some years ago when I was playing a par-5 that ran alongside a salt pond in New England. I sliced my drive over a small bank into the pond, which is a lateral hazard. I was surprised to hear in the distance something akin to a faint "thump." Had I not heard anything I would have dropped a ball at the margin and moved on, but I found that "thump" just intriguing enough to wander over to the edge of the bank and take a look. It happened to be low tide, and there, lo and behold, was my ball sitting on a tiny sliver of beach. I actually had a wide-open shot, and after hitting into the fairway I stuck my third close and made the putt for birdie. Best possible outcome, and all due to nothing more than listening. I learned that day to listen carefully to every errant shot, and this has paid off many times over the years.

How to Look for Lost Balls

By watching the ball in flight we will have noted generally where it has landed and can remember this by a nearby landmark. *The area to search should be a rectangle—two or three times as long as it is wide, centered on the landmark.* This is because the line of flight is known with far more certainty that the distance. A rectangle 15 yards wide and 40 yards long might be typical for a drive. Further insight into the distance can be gained by noting the position of the other drives and asking how well they were struck. Scan the rectangle as you approach it. Obviously the hope is that you will spot your ball from a distance and not need to do a detailed search.

The search should be done systematically so that the whole area is covered in the least amount of time. This can be done by walking the length of the rectangle along one edge, looking down, not ahead, and reversing course at the end of the rectangle and walking it in the opposite direction a few yards further into the rectangle, then repeating the process until the entire area is covered. When the ball is found, drop your hat down next to it. If it was that hard to find, don't risk losing sight of it and having to start over again. (See Diagram 2.)

If the area is so overgrown that even if the ball were to be found it would likely be unplayable, just take a penalty, drop a new ball, and move on. Rules as they apply to recreational play are addressed later in Chapter 4, where you will find suggestions for efficient and fair ways to deal with such situations.

When to Give Up Looking

Discretion must be used in deciding how long to look for a lost ball. On a crowded course when play is continuous the answer is, "Not long." Don't look to the rules for help. They say we have five minutes, but if the group behind is waiting, we will introduce a five-minute delay to that and every subsequent group for the whole day. A good rule of thumb is to stop looking within a minute after the group behind is ready to hit *and* it is your turn to hit within your own foursome. Take your medicine: Drop one and move on.

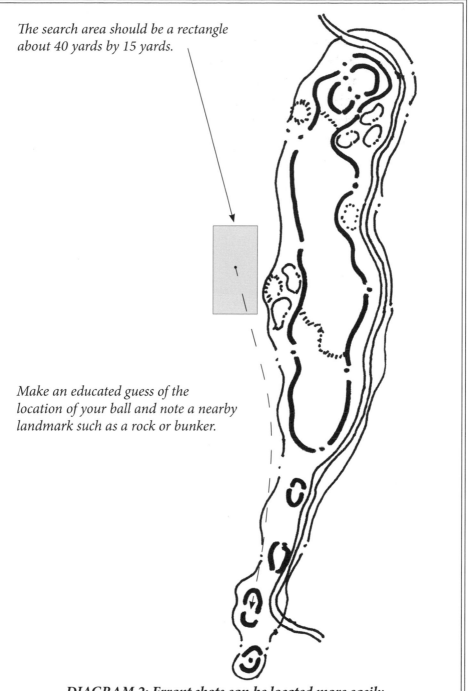

The search area should be a rectangle about 40 yards by 15 yards.

Make an educated guess of the location of your ball and note a nearby landmark such as a rock or bunker.

DIAGRAM 2: Errant shots can be located more easily if a systematic approach is taken.

Ready Golf

Being ready to hit your shot when it is your turn should be distinguished from the concept of "ready golf," which means that you can hit whenever you are ready. Ready golf carried to the extreme is chaos. As a general matter the concepts of the honor and of "away" should be observed, as these are part of the traditional structure of the game. But should the player who is supposed to be hitting isn't doing it, the next away player is free to play. I would actually put this more forcefully by saying *the next away player is obligated to hit, in the interest of fast play.* In doing so, not only will time be saved, but an example will be set for the others in the foursome. When he does this he should announce his intentions so that his partners will stay out of his line and give him a little space while he's hitting.

We Don't All Hit the Ball the Same Distance

We should be aware of the option for shorter hitters to hit from the tee or fairway before the group ahead has cleared the landing zone. This opportunity is often overlooked on par-3s because they are blindly regarded as one-shot holes. The reality is that many par-3s are simply unreachable for shorter hitters, particularly when they are playing from the back tees to stay with their group. It's vexing to arrive at the tee of a backed-up par-3 and see children sitting on a bench waiting for the green to clear, only to watch them hit shots halfway to the green. Far better to hit sooner and take the risk that by some miracle a shot might trickle onto the green while the group ahead is putting. In such case no harm is done, while the alternative is to sentence those behind to an unnecessary wait.

In the Fairway

Preparation for each shot begins as soon the previous one is hit. Getting the lay of the land is actually easier from a distance, so once a drive has come to rest we can begin to assess what the next shot will involve. Can the green be reached? If so, what line will give the best chance to avoid trouble and still leave the ball in position to make par or birdie? If the green can't be reached, what kind of lay-up will give the next shot the best chance to succeed? And so on. This process can play out as we approach the ball.

In general, after a foursome has teed off, all players should go directly to their ball. The only exceptions will be if help is required in finding another player's lost ball, or if by going to your ball you will be in another's line. These exceptions are to ensure that the foursome continues to move forward and does not need to backtrack.

If the location of your ball is not exactly known, do not detour to help a partner with a lost ball, because a foursome with two lost balls and only one search team is flirting with a time-consuming debacle. Go directly to yours and locate it.

When waiting to hit in the fairway, players can frequently carry out preparations beyond club selection and shot planning. Since they are likely some distance from their partners, they can actually take practice swings that replicate the shot they want to execute. When their turn is up, they have only to step up to the ball and hit it. Under these circumstances, 20 seconds is plenty of time to hit. (See Diagram 3.)

Go Your Separate Way

One of the pleasures of the game is walking the course with your partners. But if this takes any of you significantly out of the way, forgo it. It

Three players are standing next to a partner while he hits instead of going to their balls and preparing to hit their own shots.

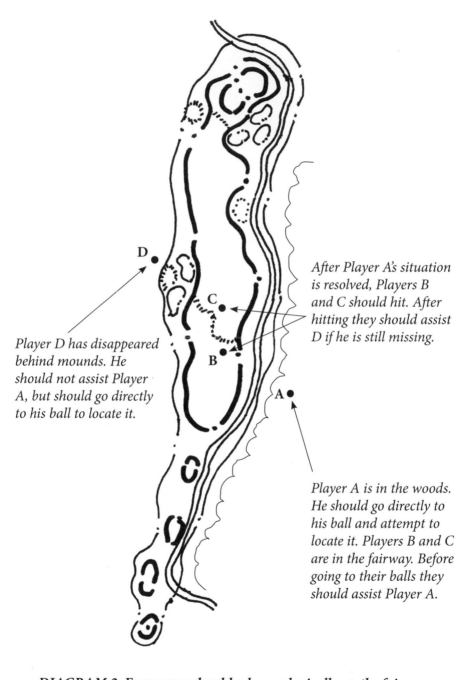

D

Player D has disappeared behind mounds. He should not assist Player A, but should go directly to his ball to locate it.

C

B

A

After Player A's situation is resolved, Players B and C should hit. After hitting they should assist D if he is still missing.

Player A is in the woods. He should go directly to his ball and attempt to locate it. Players B and C are in the fairway. Before going to their balls they should assist Player A.

DIAGRAM 3: Foursomes should advance logically up the fairway. Players with lost balls should be assisted by their partners in sequence.

obviously takes a lot more time for four golfers to walk en masse to the first player's ball, wait for that shot, walk to the next player's ball, and so on. It makes the fundamental idea of being ready to hit when it's your turn an impossibility. So walk together as long as you are proceeding to your ball, too, but peel off when it's time.

Passing Partners, Hitting out of Sequence

We should all rid ourselves forever of the notion that we need to stay behind our playing partners until they have hit. Of course we must stay out of their line, but consistent with this, we can go as far up the hole toward our ball as possible. Each member of the foursome should advance along the hole at the earliest possible opportunity. This may take you far afield, such as when you have hit a long hook off the fairway and your partner has hit a short slice, but unless you do this you will not be ready to hit when it is your turn. A bonus is that if you are well up the fairway, you become an advance scout for the foursome, as you will be in a much better position to follow their shots and to see or deduce where their balls come to rest.

When a golfer gets to his ball, he can make a judgment of whether to hit immediately or wait. The longstanding protocol of the game is to hit in sequence, but a golfer should be prepared to hit out of sequence in a number of situations:

- The golfer is in the woods or otherwise out of sight of the other players in the group.
- The golfer is one of two or more players looking for lost balls, and he finds his while the others are still looking.
- If, for any reason, the player who is away is not ready to hit.
- If the golfer cannot reach the players in the next group but his partners can.
- If the golfer is riding and playing with walkers and he reaches his ball well in advance of the walkers. In such an instance, the golfer should inform the walkers that he does not mean to be rude, but that he is hitting first in the interest of fast play. (See Diagram 4.)

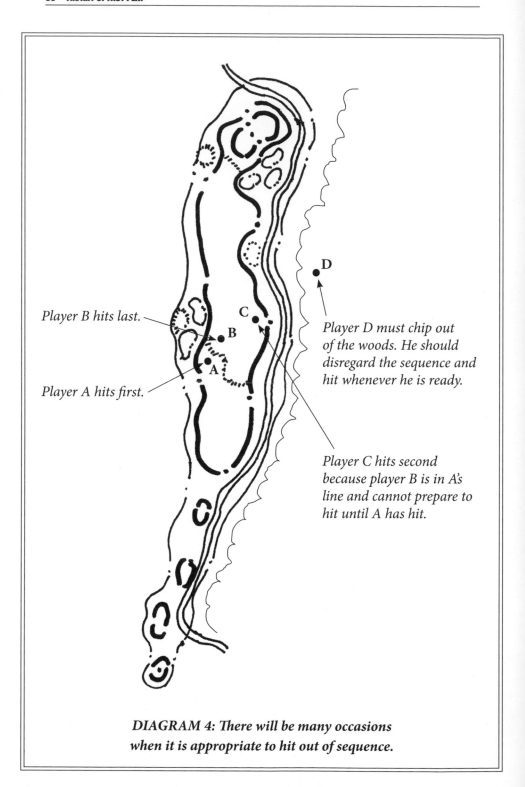

Player B hits last.

C

B

Player A hits first.

A

D

Player D must chip out of the woods. He should disregard the sequence and hit whenever he is ready.

Player C hits second because player B is in A's line and cannot prepare to hit until A has hit.

DIAGRAM 4: *There will be many occasions when it is appropriate to hit out of sequence.*

Around and on the Green

Remember that preparation begins for each shot as soon as the previous one has been hit. This is equally true as the green is approached. Once again, the lay of the land is often easier to assess from a distance. If your ball is actually on the green you know that you will be putting soon, so if you are one who routinely removes your glove to putt, do it at the first possible moment. If you don't, you may find yourself standing over your putt, having forgotten to do it, and removing it then brings things unnecessarily to a standstill.

I've observed that, with the exception of looking for lost balls, there is more potential for wasting time around and on the greens than anywhere else on the golf course. This is because all four players' balls are close together, and in the absence of protocols about how to behave, things can stall. It's actually pretty common for all four players to defer, to wait for someone else to act. Polite behavior, yes, but not the best thing for fast play.

It happens often in the immediate green environment that a player who believes he is not away is standing over his ball making practice strokes. The player who is actually away, who is also previewing his stroke, misinterprets these actions as meaning that the first player is about to hit. Both end up waiting for the other to hit. Eventually they will make eye contact and sort things out, but this is an unnecessary delay. To use a tennis expression, it's an unforced error.

Someone Has to Take Charge

The situation calls for a conductor, automatically the player whose ball is closest to the hole when the foursome arrives on the green. That golfer should mark the ball if it is in anyone's line, go to the hole to announce who is away, and tend the flag for anyone who needs it. When a putt is given, the conductor on the green should toss it aside so that play can continue immediately. When a putt isn't given but is in the way of another's line, the golfer should mark the ball and toss it to its owner. At the point when someone else's putt arrives inside his, that player should assume conducting duties. When it is time to remove the flag for good, care should be taken to lay it on the green where it will not interfere with subsequent play.

The first player to hole out becomes the conductor for the remainder of the hole. On finishing, that player should pick up the flagstick, stand out of everyone's line, and be ready to replace the flag as soon as play is concluded. This will avoid confusion about who should replace the flag and ensure that it happens right away. It will also eliminate the comical possibility of not replacing it at all. As anyone who has played golf for a while knows, this can and does happen.

Keep in mind that in the event a player in the foursome has had enough on a particular hole and picked up, that player is then available to take on the obligations of the conductor for the rest of the hole. I have found this to be a far better use of my time than sulking off and wallowing in the self-loathing that I often feel following a disastrous hole.

The player holding the flag, the "conductor," has putted out and will replace the flag as soon as play is completed.

Order of Play on the Green

As in the fairway, the concept of "away" should not be strictly applied on the greens. The most common example of this is when the away player is not ready to hit. This happens for various reasons, perhaps most frequently when a player skulls the ball out of a bunker and across the green. In such case it is silly to hold up play while he rakes the bunker, climbs out, walks across the green, locates the ball, and plans and executes his next shot. Begin play on the green and continue until your partner is ready to hit again.

As an aside, when a player skulls a shot over the green, be aware that the player who hit the shot often can't see where it winds up from his vantage point below the green in a bunker. The players waiting on the green should make a concerted effort to follow the ball until it comes to rest, and if this is in the woods or in tall grass, they should go immediately to the spot and locate the ball. Otherwise the hitter, upon emerging from the bunker, will be clueless about the ball's whereabouts, and the whole foursome will be looking for the lost ball. In such situations it is really annoying to come out of the bunker and ask where your ball is, only to find out nobody followed your shot. They'll say, "I didn't see it," but what they really mean is that they weren't unselfish enough and alert enough to watch.

In the protocol of match play the player who is away hits first, whether on the green or not. But generally players not actually on the green should volunteer to play first even though they may not be away, as this avoids repeatedly removing and replacing the flagstick. There will be exceptions to this. For example, a player may want to wait if he feels he will benefit by observing the shot of an opponent who is away. Or another player, even though he is not on the putting surface, may want the flagstick taken out, in which case nothing is gained by his going first.

Where to Put Spare Clubs

Players often arrive at the green carrying several clubs, which they lay down while putting. It happens all too often that they forget them after finishing the hole and don't discover that they are missing until a hole or two later. Few things will slow play like driving around the course looking for lost clubs.

I had lost clubs on several occasions before I stumbled on a fail-safe solution. Losing clubs can be avoided all the time by placing them on the green (not in the fringe and especially not in the rough) in line with the exit route from the hole to your cart or bag, where you will have to see them on your way to the next hole. If all the players in a foursome put all their clubs in the same vicinity along this line, the chances of noticing them will be multiplied. I don't like putting clubs on top of the flagstick, as some have recommended. This prevents the conductor from holding the flag and slows your foursome's exit from the green.

This foursome has put its spare clubs on the line they will travel when exiting the green. This will minimize the chance that one of them will leave their clubs on the green.

Marking Balls

Marking balls with coins or ball marks is time-consuming. If every player marks his ball twice on every green, a round cannot be played in four hours. Remember, each player has only 20 seconds, on average, to play each shot. A golfer cannot replace the ball, plan the line, and execute a putt in 20 seconds, and still do justice to the shot. On the other hand, a golfer can easily clean and align a ball on the green without marking it by squatting down behind the ball, placing the toe of the putter immediately next to the ball before picking it up, and keeping the putter toe on this spot (leaning the putter against his shoulder if he wants to keep both hands free) while cleaning or aligning the ball. This is not only quick but very accurate. Accordingly, balls need not be marked unless they are actually in another player's line, or if they are so close as to be a distraction. Once again, just because the pros on TV do it doesn't mean we have to do it.

This player is marking his ball with the toe of his putter while he cleans and aligns it. This takes a fraction of the time required to mark it with a coin, step away to clean it, then replace and align it.

Planning Putts

All too often players do not begin to plan or align their putts until it is actually their turn to putt. This wastes time—lots of it. Taking the game seriously requires observing one's putt from different angles, studying the line, repairing ball marks, and so forth. However, there is no reason why most of this activity cannot take place before a player's turn comes up.

The job of planning and aligning a putt begins as the green is approached. The general contour can be observed while walking onto the green; if the route taken to the ball is carefully chosen, the line from the opposite side of the hole, and the vicinity of the hole itself, can be observed before even reaching the ball. Unless you are required to putt first, or unless you are in someone's line, you can observe your putt practically at your leisure, even walking around the green to see it from differing angles while others are putting. (You need to be still only while they are actually stroking their ball.) If you are lucky enough to be in another's line, then you don't need to observe your putt from behind at all. Just watch your opponent's putt and deduce the speed and break from that shot. In short, unless you are required to putt first, you have ample time to do all the study and planning necessary to do justice to any putt—all without causing any delay to your partners at all.

The player on the right's ball is in place, and he is studying his putt while one of his partners is putting. When his turn arrives he will be ready to putt without delay.

Maximum Strokes

Unless your foursome is playing a match in which every score will be meaningful on a particular hole, players should pick up when they have reached the maximum under their handicap range. If you don't have a handicap, and most golfers don't, then set a number as your limit. It should be eight or less. A snowman is at least a triple bogey, and let's face it, anything beyond this isn't going to be terribly meaningful.

The golfing fraternity begs you to never agree to a stroke-play format, especially one where you have to putt everything out. You can imagine the extra time required for ordinary players to finish every hole to the bitter end, even when they have completely lost it.

SUMMARY: When It's Your Turn, Be Ready to Hit

- On average, you have 20 seconds to hit your shot from the time it is your turn. If your group takes 30 seconds per shot, it will add an hour to your round.
- Don't start a conversation or a joke on the tee if the fairway is open. When the fairway is clear, golf must be the first order of business.
- Always know who has the honor. If it is you, go directly to the tee box and prepare to hit.
- If it is not you, and no one takes the tee box, announce that someone has to hit and you will do it in the interest of time.
- Watch and listen intently to each shot—both yours and your playing partners'.
- Short hitters should hit as soon as the group ahead is out of their range, regardless of the honor.
- After your group has teed off, go directly to your ball unless a partner needs help in finding a ball, or unless you are in someone's line.
- Do not help a partner find a ball unless the whereabouts of yours is known.
- Be prepared to hit out of sequence if the player who is away is not ready or able to hit.

- When your foursome is on the green, the player closest to the hole at any given time becomes a conductor, deciding who is away and tending the flag.
- The first player to hole out should hold the flag for the remainder of play, replacing it immediately upon completion of the hole.
- Generally, players who are off the green should hit first, regardless of who is away.
- Put spare clubs on the green on the exit route between the hole and your bag or cart.
- You do not need to mark your ball unless you are in someone's line or so close to their line as to be a distraction. You can clean and align your ball without marking it by placing the toe of your putter on the spot.
- Plan and align your putts as you approach the green and while others are putting.
- Pick up when you have reached the maximum under your handicap range or, if you don't have a handicap, after no more than eight shots.

CHAPTER 4

Treat the Rules of Golf with Discretion

"In an attempt to speed up play, a local rule option will allow changing out-of-bounds stakes to lateral hazards."
—AN (UNFULFILLED) PREDICTION BY GARY WREN MADE IN 2003

"That's the beauty of water hazards. There's no searching . . . only cursing, dropping, and hitting."
—JOHN WEYLER

THE RULES OF GOLF form the basis for the conduct of the ancient game. They are lengthy and complex, but this is a necessity in an honor system. Since there are no referees in golf there can be no gray areas and no judgment calls. The USGA and the Royal and Ancient together have done a remarkable job of this in their written rules and decisions that have evolved over centuries.

No one thinking straight would want to discard this special system. Similarly, no one would want a match in a Sunday foursome to be conducted with the same strict adherence to the rules found in a professional tournament. The spirit of the rules should not be violated, but certain accommodations need to be made in the interest of faster play. Otherwise a friendly Sunday game can take on a stilted, bureaucratic character marked by pointless delays and a focus on minutiae.

Lost Balls and Out of Bounds

Some may consider this heresy, but I believe that the rules regarding lost balls and balls hit out of bounds are simply impractical for recreational play. Without question, they are devastating to speed of play.

It all begins with the concept of the provisional ball, which asks a player to hit a second shot if there is a chance of not finding the first. Touring pros aren't in this situation too often, but the everyday player is in it all the time. Upon electing to hit a provisional, a player is in the immediate position of trying to find two balls. The rules allow five minutes to locate the first one—a maddening delay to playing partners and those waiting on the tee. Whether the first ball is found or not, the player still must locate and retrieve (or hit) the second ball. Since it is precisely the poorer player who is in this position, and since Murphy's Law is immutable, the second ball is invariably on the opposite side of the hole. The situation becomes truly comical if the second ball cannot be found or if the player has misjudged the quality of the original shot and failed to hit a provisional. In either event the golfer must return to the tee or to the place of the previous shot (where was that, exactly?) and hit again.

I recently observed an absurd turn of events in a tournament: A player hit a tee shot that disappeared into woods and was likely to be lost, so he hit a provisional. After a lengthy search the original ball was located in a thicket. It was totally unplayable, and the relief offered by the rules for unplayable lies was of no use. He couldn't find an open spot within two club lengths, and moving backward on the line to the flag took him out of bounds. The only remaining option was to return to the tee and hit again. Yes, he had to walk back to the tee and hit yet another drive—*his third!*—the provisional shot having been rendered moot by finding his first one. The whole debacle took 15 minutes or more, and set the entire tournament back the equivalent of at least one entire hole. For every following group it was like driving down a freeway and coming to dead standstill because an accident had blocked the road. If this scenario played out at a public golf course I'd worry about the safety of the person causing it.

The system is unworkable for recreational play. Many have discovered this on their own. Unless they are playing in a tournament or in a money match of epic proportions, many players, aware of the intolerable delays imposed on their innocent partners or on other groups, won't walk back to the tee or even spend the five minutes they are allowed. More often than not a player will simply say, "I'll drop one here," and move on. This disrespect for the rule is inevitable. The rule is unworkable.

Further, as a matter of simple fairness the punishment doesn't fit the crime. I realize that golf is a cruel game with Calvinist roots and that the concept of "rub of the green" is deeply ingrained in the sport. However, there can be no logical reason for why hitting a ball into rough, or woods, or across a neighboring fence, or merely under an autumn leaf should carry essentially twice the penalty as hitting it into some totally unredeemable place like a swamp or a river or the ocean. A stroke is a precious thing. No rule should be as wildly capricious as this.

It is doubly vexing in situations, all too common nowadays, where the only reason for a penalty is that a ball has come to rest, in a perfectly playable lie, beyond a row of out-of-bounds stakes alongside a housing development that is built too close to the course in the first place.

I think it is reasonable to suggest that recreational play be distinguished from tournament play in one significant way: Play would be speeded and simplified if we could adopt a concept of the "last known point" in the journey of a golf ball. In the new world I have dared to envision, this, by definition, would be the place along its flight line where it crossed over or into the woods (using the drip line of the trees as a margin), where it disappeared into deep grass or a thicket, or where it crossed an out-of-bounds line. Such situations would be treated like lateral hazards—a ball would be dropped within two club lengths of this "last known point," no nearer the hole, with a one-stroke penalty. Unless the ball is out of bounds, a player would still have the option of locating the original shot and hitting it, much as a golfer may elect to play from a hazard if the ball is findable and hittable.

It is baffling that the rules require a low standard of certainty about balls hit into hazards, but an utterly exacting standard when they're not. Although a ball hit into a water hazard is definitely "lost," it isn't treated as such. It is only necessary to know that the ball went into the hazard and to make an educated guess about where it crossed the margin to justify a one-stroke penalty. On the other hand, if a ball is not hit into a hazard, it must be actually located and identified to escape the dreaded penalty of stroke and distance. Let's be honest: This is arbitrary and inconsistent.

When a ball is hit off the fairway in the woods or grass, the player and the rest of the foursome observe the ball's flight and have a pretty decent idea of where it went. It's not on Mars, after all. True, we might not know exactly where it is, but we do know it went into the woods or flew into the tall grass. We know this with at least the same degree of certainty that we hold when a ball flies into a lake. We can estimate its flight line with the same degree of accuracy.

If the concept of "last known point" could be adopted for recreational play, it would immediately make a fairer, less arbitrary, and most important, much faster game. The hated phrase "stroke and distance" could be eliminated from the golfing lexicon, as could the time-consuming use of provisional balls. (See Diagram 5.)

Finding Balls

Let's say your opponent has hit the ball into the woods and you are helping with the search. As often happens when a shot is heard to rattle around in the woods, there is a large area where the ball might have come to rest. As also often happens in this situation, several balls might be found during the search. Let's say you spot a ball that is partially buried in some leaves, but you can't see the identifying marks. Your opponent is 40 yards away on the other side of a thicket. Technically you must wait for him to come over and identify it. If it turns out to be his ball, well and good, but if not, you are back to square one and you resume the search. The group on the tee behind, seeing all this activity, is seething.

It would be common sense to pick up the ball, identify it, and yell across the woods to your opponent to ask what ball he's playing. If it's his, you place it back where you found it, wait for him to arrive so that you don't run the risk of losing sight of it, and continue to play the hole. If it's not his, you add it to your larder and continue to look. Is it a violation of a sacred trust? No, it's just common sense. In a tournament, where a lot is at stake, you should not pick up the ball because the burden of replacing it exactly as it was found lies with the player who hit the shot.

As for the five minutes you are allowed to look, it's way too long if people are waiting, as we discussed in chapter 3.

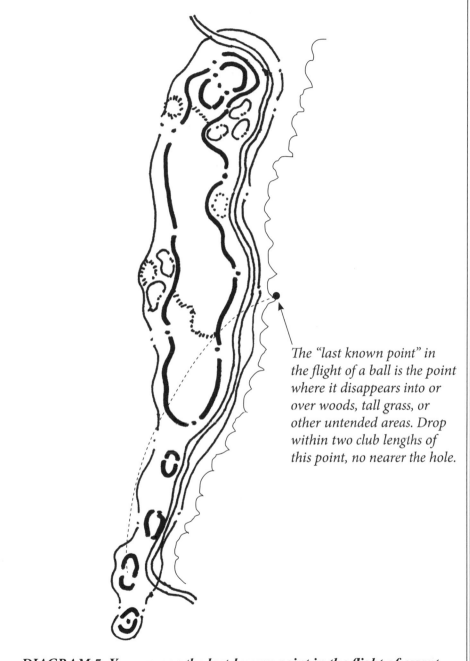

The "last known point" in the flight of a ball is the point where it disappears into or over woods, tall grass, or other untended areas. Drop within two club lengths of this point, no nearer the hole.

DIAGRAM 5: *You can use the last-known point in the flight of errant shots as the margin of a lateral hazard in lieu of hitting provisional balls. If you can't find the ball, take a one-stroke penalty and move on.*

Mark Your Playing Partners' Balls

Your foursome should make a regular habit of marking each other's balls when this can save time. Let's say you are on the green and your opponent, in a bunker 30 yards away, hits a beautiful shot that comes to rest inside your ball and on the line to the hole. Do you wait for your opponent to rake the bunker, walk to the green, and mark the ball? Or do you mark it, remove the flag, and proceed to putt? In a tournament there is logic to the former, but not in a Sunday foursome. Similarly, many long putts come to rest in someone else's line, and in such cases it only makes sense for a player who is close by to reach down and mark it. Many players don't know that the rules actually allow this, providing you have your opponent's permission.

Unraked Bunkers

We all know we are supposed to play the ball where it lies. However, in the case where a previous player has ignored the etiquette of raking a bunker and you wind up in a footprint or ball mark, an adjustment seems necessary in the interest of fairness and time. I suggest your group adopt the following procedure: Pick up the ball, rake out the footprint, and drop the ball in the newly raked area. True, this will take a few seconds, but far less time than the multishot debacle that can follow an attempt to hit out of a footprint.

"Leaf Balls"

In the autumn it's inevitable that many balls in perfectly playable places go unfound because they have drifted under a fallen leaf. It seems reasonable that when the vicinity of a shot is known with certainty, but that spot is littered with autumn leaves, you and your partners could agree to declare this a "leaf ball," which would lead to a free drop and a timely resumption of play.

Tending the Flag

The rules say that you are penalized if your putt hits the flagstick. But what if you are on the green, 90 feet from the pin, and your partners are all busy raking bunkers and such, and people behind are waiting to hit.

In the interest of time and fairness, your group might agree that in the event a ball winds up in a footprint, you will rake out the footprint and drop the ball into the freshly raked area.

Are you really going to wait for one of them to get around to tending the flag? A better solution is to ask if they will waive the pin rule in this one instance, in which case you can just go ahead and putt. The chances are minuscule that you will actually hit the pin, and if you do, no real harm is done.

Away

In match play, and thankfully most recreational play is done in a match-play format, the player who is away hits first. We've discussed how this shouldn't be observed obsessively in the fairway. Nor should it be on and around the greens when others are waiting. Say your opponent is in a bunker and is still away after hitting to the green. Are you really going to wait while your opponent rakes the bunker, walks onto the green, cleans the ball, studies the line, and finally putts it? No, you are going to putt out of order to keep things moving and to give your opponent a chance to breathe.

It is a matter of common sense to make adjustments such as these in the strict application of the rules. They speed up play and have no real effect on the outcome of the match.

SUMMARY: Treat the Rules of Golf with Discretion

- Consider treating woods, tall grass, and other untended areas as lateral hazards.
- Don't be afraid to remove and identify an opponent's ball.
- Make a routine practice of marking an opponent's ball when it will save time.
- Putt to an untended flag when the group behind is waiting and no one is available to tend the pin.
- Don't obsessively adhere to the concept of "away" when others are waiting.
- Make reasonable accommodations to ensure fair and timely play when arbitrary course conditions, such as untended bunkers and unraked autumn leaves, interfere with play.

CHAPTER 5

Operate Carts as a Team

*"Ninety-three percent of recreational golfers say
slow play detracts from their enjoyment of the game."*
—*Golf* MAGAZINE POLL

MOTORIZED CARTS HAVE BECOME a way of life in public golf, not so much because they are faster, but because they reduce the endurance required to play. Walking five miles in hot weather on a hilly course is a workout, plain and simple, and many people just aren't up to it. Some courses, usually in real estate developments, have long distances between greens and tees. Just one or two of these long transitions can render a course unwalkable.

For these reasons (and because carts are a big source of revenue for courses) they are here to stay. But they are not a panacea to slow play. A cart can't be in two places at once, so one of the occupants just sits and waits a lot of the time. And because carts are severely limited in where they can actually go, golfers are forever getting in and out of them, which leads to much confusion as to who should reposition the cart, and where. It isn't that unusual for golfers to actually forget their cart. They both get out with a selection of clubs and, following a string of disappointing shots, wind up on the green, each assuming that the other is worrying about the cart. Once they have finished the hole they realize that the cart is still 75 yards back down the fairway. As Dave Barry might say, I am not making this up.

Don't Be Seduced by the Apparent Speed of Carts

My foursome recently took advantage of a sunny, windless day in January to play a nearby daily-fee course. It was an ordinary weekday, and with the temperature in the low 40s the course was virtually deserted. We were walking, and as all winter golfers know, walking will raise the effective temperature on the course by 10 to 15 degrees, making such a day more than comfortable. It can be a special experience playing on a deserted course on a good winter day.

We teed off in obscurity and for four or five holes we rollicked along at a good pace. But on emerging from a wooded part of the course onto the tee of a par-3, we confronted a foursome in carts. Two couples, bundled up like Eskimos, were on the green. We could see that no one was in front of them. On foot we had overtaken a group in carts. Annoying, yes, but with the course deserted we figured we would play through and be on our way.

It was not to be. They ignored us, and there wasn't a ranger in sight. We waited on every shot, but because we were on foot we could never get close enough to them to ask to play through. We stood on the tee and in the fairway for over five hours waiting and waiting. Since they couldn't take the carts off the paths they were forever at a loss. They would walk across the fairway without a club, one assumes in order to find their ball, so they could then return to the cart to obtain the appropriate club, so that they could then return to their ball and hit it, so that they could then return to the cart. But often as not they would hit it only a little way, which caused them to walk back to the cart to obtain another club so that they could walk back across the fairway to hit it again. In the process they never advanced the cart so that when they finally hit a good one the cart was way behind them. This happened repeatedly.

After the round this group was in the bar and we overheard one of them say, looking at his watch, "That wasn't too bad at all." On hearing this, the anger bubbled over, and collectively we took issue. "Not too bad for you maybe, but did it ever occur to you that we were forced to watch the entire fiasco?" "We waited on every shot." "Why didn't you let us play through?" "Five hours in the dead of winter, that's totally ridiculous."

On hearing this they were flabbergasted. It was obvious they had absolutely no idea that we had waited for them. "I'm sorry," one of them said, looking puzzled, "but weren't you walking? Yes, you were walking. We were riding in carts. We were always way ahead of you, weren't we?" Now it was our turn to be flabbergasted. "No," I said, "we waited on every shot."

This experience was frustrating beyond belief, but it did provide an object lesson about slow play. These people had no idea that they were holding us up. Their situational awareness was nonexistent, true, but something else was going on: The apparent speed of their carts had destroyed their perspective.

They could sense that we were behind them, but as they sped away after hitting their shots the sudden distance put between us gave them a false sense of the speed of their play. They could not fathom that walkers could actually be held up by golfers riding in carts. Such is the paradox of motorized carts.

When golfers walk and carry or pull their own bags, straight-line geometry is on their side. They can go directly to the ball over almost any terrain, put the bag down, and hit the shot. Walkers are never restricted to a cart path. They can take a golf bag into the woods, to the edge of a bunker, to the edge of the green. There is no wasted motion. The full complement of equipment is immediately at hand in the event they are surprised by what they find. The possibilities for mismanaging this simple system are remote.

On the other hand, motorized carts are frequently mismanaged on the golf course. This isn't from stupidity or incompetence; it's from not knowing any better. There is no opportunity in the process of learning how to play golf to learn how to use a cart efficiently. We're given the key and sent into the fray. It takes 30 seconds to learn to *operate* one, but as evidenced by what we have all witnessed, a lifetime isn't necessarily enough to learn how to *use* one.

Working as a Team

Since there are two of you in the cart you should operate as a team. The person whose bag is placed on the left-hand side should do most of the driving so that the two of you aren't constantly bumping into each other as you retrieve your clubs from the rear of the cart. But this does not mean that if you are riding shotgun you will never drive. On the contrary, there will be many occasions when you will need to drive the cart.

And just because you are in golf carts doesn't mean you will never need to walk. In fact, to play efficiently you will often walk for short distances and occasionally even for long ones.

The overriding principle of teamwork in carts is that both golfers are doing something to advance the round whenever possible. As we shall see, this often requires one of the occupants to get out and walk.

There should be few times when one player is sitting idle in the cart waiting for the other to hit. After teeing off you should drive to the shortest ball. Let's say it's yours. You should get out and select a club. If you are unsure, you should pull two or three clubs. In the normal instance your partner should then drive to his ball (staying out of your line, of course), leaving you to plan and execute your shot. After hitting, you should start walking up the fairway to rejoin him after he has hit his shot.

Carts are not as fast as walking unless they are used properly. The player sitting in the cart should have moved over to the driver's seat and driven to his own ball instead of just sitting and watching his partner hit.

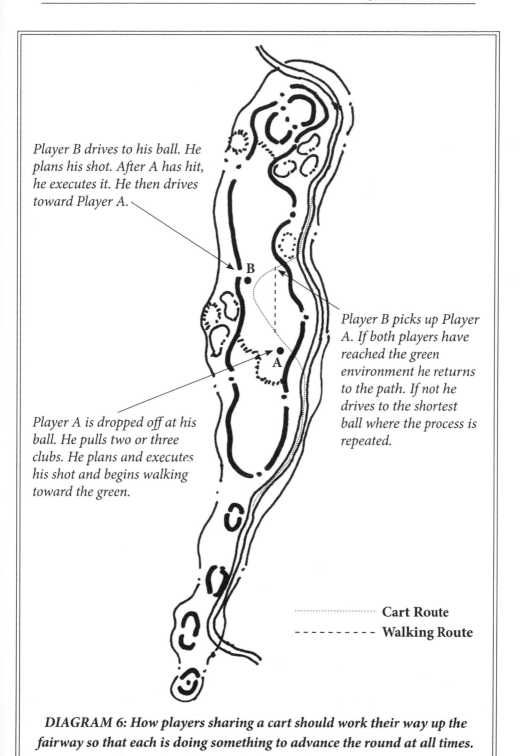

Player B drives to his ball. He plans his shot. After A has hit, he executes it. He then drives toward Player A.

Player B picks up Player A. If both players have reached the green environment he returns to the path. If not he drives to the shortest ball where the process is repeated.

Player A is dropped off at his ball. He pulls two or three clubs. He plans and executes his shot and begins walking toward the green.

B

A

············· **Cart Route**

- - - - - - - - - **Walking Route**

DIAGRAM 6: How players sharing a cart should work their way up the fairway so that each is doing something to advance the round at all times.

Exceptions

There are three exceptions to the normal policy of dropping one player off and driving to the other's ball.

- When one of you has topped a drive and the other's ball is more than, say, 75 yards ahead, you should wait for the shorter player to hit. A player who has topped it once might top it again, and in such case, who knows what club will be needed?
- If one is in the other's line, you obviously must wait.
- If your balls are close to each other, you can get out together. Repositioning the cart is wasted motion if the alternative is available for one of you to walk 20 or 30 yards to the ball while the other is hitting.

When players have hit their drives in the same vicinity, the cart can be parked between them and both players can hit without having to reposition the cart.

When Carts Are Confined to the Paths

Riding in carts that are confined to the paths is a wretched way to play golf. It changes the game fundamentally. Instead of moving along the course in a linear and sequential way, we are forced to play it side-to-side, herky-jerky, and something more than perspective is lost. In bad weather it's understandable, but it's unfortunate that some courses have made a permanent operational decision to keep carts off the course.

Teamwork is even more essential when carts are confined to the paths. If your ball is shortest off the tee, your partner should drop you off and drive up the path, parking plainly ahead of his own ball position. The reason he should pull ahead is to ensure that after hitting he will be walking forward, clearing the landing zone and moving toward the green. *Always err on the side of taking the cart too far.* After you have hit, walk toward the cart. You and your partner may join there and proceed up the fairway or to the green, or if your partner has strayed far afield it may be essential for you to take the cart alone the rest of the way to the green. It may also be necessary for you to meet him in the fairway on foot with one of his clubs, if for any reason he finds himself with the wrong equipment. If ever there's a time for teamwork, this is it.

Often the scenario will develop where one of you will intentionally drive alone to the green from as far as 200 yards away. Let's say that on a par-4 your drives are both in play. Your partner's ball is next to the cart path, but yours is in the opposite rough, 70 yards away. In such event you should pull all the clubs you might need to get to the green (assume you will hit a bad one along the way), plus your putter. This allows you to clear the landing zone immediately after hitting your shot, meaning those behind will be spared watching you walk all the way back across the hole to the cart. At a minimum you should walk at an angle up the fairway to rejoin the cart. But depending on terrain, distance, and the location of your partner, you might choose to walk all the way to the green, as that will involve less time and effort than getting back to the cart.

As you may have noticed, it's not a perfect world. There will be times when you are both on the opposite side of the course from the cart path, and there is no efficient way to get the cart to the green. Make the best of it. If you have hit your shot closer to the green than your partner, hustle back across the fairway and move the cart forward. If the group behind has been treated to a long wait you might think of jogging across the fairway. This will save a little time and it will send a signal that you are aware you are having a slow hole and are doing the best you can. Another option is for one of the other players in the group to drive your cart to the green. (See *Driving an Opponent's Cart*, page 64)

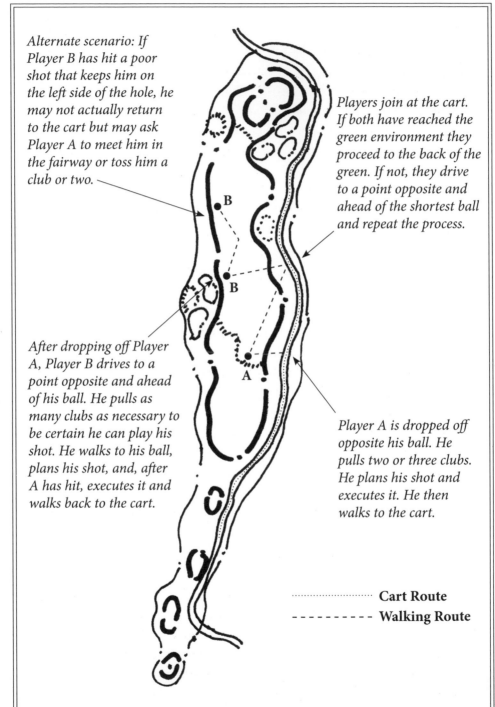

Alternate scenario: If Player B has hit a poor shot that keeps him on the left side of the hole, he may not actually return to the cart but may ask Player A to meet him in the fairway or toss him a club or two.

Players join at the cart. If both have reached the green environment they proceed to the back of the green. If not, they drive to a point opposite and ahead of the shortest ball and repeat the process.

After dropping off Player A, Player B drives to a point opposite and ahead of his ball. He pulls as many clubs as necessary to be certain he can play his shot. He walks to his ball, plans his shot, and, after A has hit, executes it and walks back to the cart.

Player A is dropped off opposite his ball. He pulls two or three clubs. He plans his shot and executes it. He then walks to the cart.

B

B

A

.... **Cart Route**

- - - - - - - - - **Walking Route**

DIAGRAM 7: Teamwork is required whenever carts are confined to the path.

Similar Situations

Even when carts are not confined to the paths there are situations where they might as well be. For example, when the path is on the right-hand side of the hole and you have pull-hooked your approach shot to the left of the green, you might as well pull what I'll call your "greenside clubs"—for most players, a putter, a sand or lob wedge, and a chipping club such as a 9-iron—and just walk to your ball. It's probably not any further than walking from the cart after it's parked on the opposite side of the green, and it's a lot faster because your partner can proceed alone in the cart, saving a time-consuming detour to the other side of the hole. (See Diagram 8.)

On par-3s (where carts are routinely confined to the path) we should take the same strategy when our approach winds up on the opposite side of the hole from the path. Anytime we can walk to our ball as easily as riding to it, we should take the walking option, because that leaves our partner in the cart with only one person to worry about.

Riding Ahead

Use the mobility of the cart to help the foursome play efficiently. For example, if you and your partner have both hit your second shots on a par-4, but your opponents have not yet hit, there is little point in waiting for them to execute their shots when you could race ahead in the cart (well out of their line, of course) and get in a position to watch their shots. If one of them hits a bad one, this could save you a lot of time in locating it. After they have hit you can proceed from your vantage point immediately to your ball or to the green and prepare for your next shot. You can also use the cart to scout blind shots and to see if the green is clear. (See Diagram 9.)

Carts can be used to help walkers who have been paired with riders. If you observe that a walking opponent has hit a bad shot that will take some effort to find, don't wait for the player to reach the ball. Assuming it doesn't take you into someone's line, make a beeline in the cart to the trouble spot and begin searching for the ball. Similarly, if you are paired with beginners, you can use the cart to help search for their balls and still get to your own in good time. If you don't help out in these cases you will find yourself sitting and waiting for them to find and hit their balls. Waiting like this is always frustrating. Why not take the initiative to help out, which will ease that frustration and save your group a lot of time?

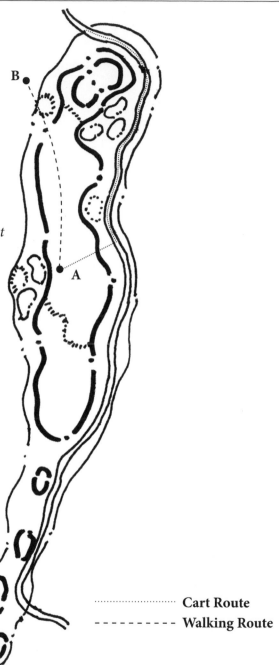

If you were in Position A and pull-hooked your shot to Position B, you might as well pull your three "greenside" clubs and walk to your ball. Then your partner can take the cart directly to the green without any detour.

B

A

·············· **Cart Route**

‑ ‑ ‑ ‑ ‑ ‑ ‑ ‑ **Walking Route**

DIAGRAM 8: Take advantage of opportunities to walk to your ball when riding will take your partner on a significant detour.

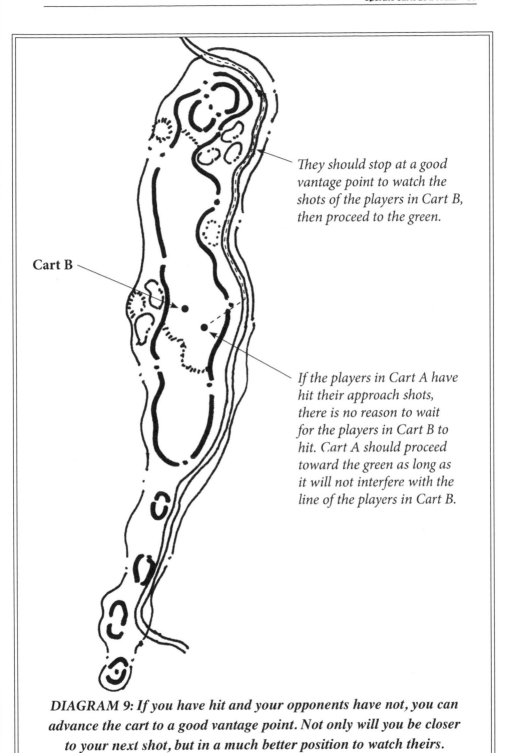

They should stop at a good vantage point to watch the shots of the players in Cart B, then proceed to the green.

Cart B

If the players in Cart A have hit their approach shots, there is no reason to wait for the players in Cart B to hit. Cart A should proceed toward the green as long as it will not interfere with the line of the players in Cart B.

DIAGRAM 9: If you have hit and your opponents have not, you can advance the cart to a good vantage point. Not only will you be closer to your next shot, but in a much better position to watch theirs.

Driving an Opponent's Cart

We should always be aware of the position on the course of everyone in the foursome, especially when carts are confined to the paths. Remember, since a foursome has four drivers and only two carts, we have extra drivers to help get the carts to the green when players get caught a long way from theirs. Obviously we need to be alert and see the whole picture to take advantage of this. If you see a situation develop that has taken both occupants of a cart to the opposite side of the course, and you are nearby, volunteer to take their cart to the green. Conversely, if you and your partner find yourselves on the opposite side of the course from the path, ask one of your opponents to drive yours up to the green.

Singles in Carts

It often happens that riders will occur in threesomes, which brings about the special case of a single in a cart. It is likely that at some point during the round the single will need help in moving his cart. This will be a certainty if the carts are confined to the paths. If you are in a twosome, be alert to this fact and volunteer to reposition the single's cart when he is far from the path. He will be grateful for your help, it will speed play for all of you, and as a bonus, you will have introduced him to a fast-play technique that he can use in the future.

SUMMARY: Operate Carts as a Team

- ♀ Don't be seduced into thinking you are playing fast simply because you are in a cart. If not handled properly, play in carts can be slower than walking.
- ♀ To play fast in carts you must work as a team. Drop one player off at his ball and proceed to the other so that both you and your partner can be doing something to advance the round at all times.
- ♀ Try to never get a cart into a position where it must backtrack.
- ♀ When carts are confined to the paths and your ball is across the fairway, be prepared to walk to the green after hitting in lieu of walking back across the fairway while the group behind is waiting.

☙ Always err on the side of taking the cart too far up the path, as this will ensure that you are always walking toward the hole after hitting your shots.

☙ Anytime you can walk to your ball as easily as riding to it, take the option of walking, providing your partner doesn't need you to drive.

☙ If you and your partner have hit before your opponents, ride ahead to a place where you can observe their shots.

☙ Be aware of the need to drive your opponents' cart if they are caught far from the path.

CHAPTER 6

Never Be away from the Cart with the Wrong Club

"I once watched a golfer walk 75 yards from the cart path to examine his ball, which was lying in the rough 300 yards from the green, walk 75 yards back to the cart to get a club, walk 75 yards back to his ball, and top the ball 50 yards forward."
— DAVID OWEN

AN ENORMOUS AMOUNT OF TIME is wasted when we have go back and forth to the cart to retrieve the correct club. Such behavior is always preceded by leaving the cart with the wrong club, or worse, no club at all. This brand of delay is totally avoidable with a little planning.

In the Fairway

When dropped off by your partner at your ball, take a moment to conceptualize your shot. If there is any doubt at all about the club you will play, take two or even three clubs and send your partner on his way. This way you can do the detailed planning to make your selection without delaying play.

After you return to the cart, get ready for your next shot. If you know you are on the green, grab your putter right away and hold it as you drive to the green. If you have dumped your shot into a bunker fronting the green, grab your sand wedge and your putter. Your partner can drop you with no delay as you pass the front of the green.

In the Green Environment

At some point as the fairway approaches the green, carts will be directed onto the cart path. Since it is unlikely that both you and your partner will have hit the green, it will fall to one of you to take the cart up to the green while the other pulls an assortment of clubs—every possible club, assuming the worst—to finish the hole. At this point, *the cart is not coming back*, and it is your responsibility to have the clubs you need to finish the hole. If you are anywhere close to the green, your three greenside clubs will usually suffice.

Carts are being directed off the fairway. This player's ball is well inside the sign. He has removed two wedges and a putter from his bag before his partner drives the cart to the green. He will play the remainder of the hole on foot.

After Parking at the Green

Upon parking the cart, the player who has driven up to the green yet who is not actually on the green should take every club possibly needed to finish the hole. It is very easy to be fooled by the appearance of balls near the green. Often from a distance a ball will look to be in the fringe close to the green. The player will think, "I'll just putt it," and walk with a putter as much as 40 yards to the other side of the green, only to find the ball is fully 10 yards off and can't be putted. Or the ball is off the green and the player walks to the ball with a putter and a 9-iron thinking of a chip, only to discover that the grass that looked so inviting from 100 feet away is actually four inches deep and a lob wedge is the right club. In either case, the player has just committed *the cardinal sin of being away from the cart with the wrong club*, even though the ball was only a few yards away.

This player has only his putter with him. His ball is just off the green and was in full view from the cart on the other side of the green, yet it cannot be putted because the grass is too high. Players should guard against this possibility by taking extra clubs to any ball that is not actually on the green.

When Carts Are Confined to the Paths

The problem of pulling the right club increases exponentially when the carts are confined to the paths. It needs to be said even more emphatically when carts are on the paths that *a golfer leaving the cart must always take every club conceivably required to play the shot.* This will almost always be three clubs: the first choice, plus one on each side of it. It is very easy to be fooled by the illusions of terrain and the geometry of doglegs when a ball is even a short distance from the path. You should pull three clubs to be sure. If your ball is on the opposite side of the course from the path, three clubs will likely not be enough. If you can see your ball you should still take extra clubs so that you will have the right club in the event you hit a poor shot that takes you even farther from the path.

Carts are confined to the path. This player has pulled three clubs to be sure she has the correct one. Her partner will continue up the path to his ball. The cart isn't coming back.

Take Your Whole Bag

After a couple of debacles on the opposite side of the fairway I finally realized how to handle it. I was on the left side of the fairway opposite the cart path. I took the requisite three clubs but instead of hitting the soaring iron onto the green that I had envisioned, I hit a nasty little hook. Suddenly I was *really* far from the cart path and didn't have any of the things I needed to finish the hole. The delay visited upon my partners and the foursome behind really got my attention.

I realized that no matter how ridiculous it sounded, it could actually be easier to grab my entire bag and carry it across the fairway. How many clubs can you carry before they start spilling out of your arms? How long does it take to remove and replace them? What about the increased chance of leaving one behind somewhere in this scenario? I decided that in the future I would take the way of least resistance. If you take your whole bag, then at least you know you can finish the hole with the right equipment, and without delaying everyone else.

When you do this, you and your partner need to be aware that you are essentially abandoning the cart to your partner, who will need to get it to the green with no assistance from you, regardless of what happens on the way.

Carts are confined to the paths, and this player's ball is in an unknown location on the other side of the hole. He is taking his entire bag. This way he will be certain of having the right club for his shot, and also any subsequent shots should it be necessary to finish the hole without returning to the cart.

On the Tee

It may sound counterintuitive, but often it's necessary to take several clubs to the tee. This occurs most often on par-3s. In many situations because of terrain, your cart will be parked some distance away from the actual tee placement and it won't be possible to deduce the yardage or the preferred shot from the cart. This will happen when tees are elevated and the markers can't be seen, when the teeing ground is very large, or when the geometry of the hole cannot be observed without actually standing on the tee.

In such cases, depending on the distance from the cart to the teeing ground, it will be more efficient to take several clubs onto the tee where you can make your selection without going back to the cart.

This practice will also be needed at times on par-4s and par-5s. As we all know, driver is not automatically the default selection on 4s and 5s. On short, tricky par-4s the smarter selection could easily be a hybrid or even an iron. On par-5s that are not reachable in two shots (that describes most

5s for us mortals) driver may be unnecessary, or even unwise due to the location of hazards or fairway bottlenecks designed to punish the unwary. Almost no one hits driver with the same accuracy as other clubs. Accordingly it is far more likely that hitting driver will lead to searching for lost balls or multiple recovery shots from rough or bunkers. Why hit driver if no advantage is gained?

SUMMARY: Never Be away from the Cart with the Wrong Club

- ☻ Never leave a cart without taking a club with you to play your shot.
- ☻ If you are not absolutely sure what you need, take two or three clubs and send your partner ahead.
- ☻ When dropped off near the green, take all the clubs you could possibly need to finish the hole, including a putter, sand wedge, and chipping club.
- ☻ When parked at the green, unless your ball is definitely on the putting surface, take chipping and pitching clubs in addition to your putter.
- ☻ When carts are confined to the path, take three clubs to your ball even if it is plainly visible in the fairway. If its location is unknown, take more than three—enough to be absolutely sure that you can play the shot without returning to the cart. If the ball is on the opposite side of the fairway, consider taking your whole bag so that you don't need to return to the cart at all.
- ☻ Take a selection of clubs to the tee if the actual yardage and strategic situation cannot be deduced from the cart. Be aware that on par-4s and par-5s there may be sensible alternatives to the driver. In such situations take other clubs to the tee in addition to your driver.

CHAPTER 7

Always Take Carts and Bags to the Rear of the Green

"I think after four hours you should pick up your ball and walk in."
— COLIN MONTGOMERIE

MISPARKING CARTS AT THE GREEN is a major villain in slow rounds. If properly positioned, the group behind can hit up as soon as your four-some walks off the green. If not, they must wait until you walk to the carts, put clubs away, get in the carts, and drive the remaining distance to the rear of the green, assuming no additional delay in the form of wiping down clubs before putting them away, replacing putter covers, and so on. The delay is pretty intolerable considering that it is so easily avoided.

When to Park at the Green

As the green is approached, the character of the landscape and the shots required to negotiate it undergo a change. Off the tee and in the fairway where long distances are covered in open terrain, play is relatively more suitable for motorized carts. Nearing the green, carts become less efficient until, in the immediate green environment, they are useless. There comes a moment when it is time to move the cart to its proper parking place behind the green and play the remainder of the hole on foot.

Unless you have hit your approach shot onto the green, this moment will occur before your ball has reached the putting surface, quite possibly when it is as much as 50 yards from the front of the green, which may be fully 75 yards from the center. This is the beginning of the "green environment."

This probably sounds absurdly inconvenient. You might be asked to drive behind the green, pull a handful of clubs, and walk more than 50 yards back to your ball.

I remember clearly the moment when the geometry of this situation first hit home to me. I had hit two good shots on a par-5. My playing partner had left the cart to me since he was off in the woods. My ball was on the left side of the fairway about 60 yards from the pin. Because of some big cross bunkers and steep terrain, the carts had been directed off the right side of the fairway and onto the path some 100 yards from the green. I blindly parked on the path opposite my ball and walked about 50 yards across the fairway to hit my third shot. I promptly hit a munch that went about halfway to the green. I walked after it and this time was able to get it onto the green. It wasn't until I walked onto the green that I realized the cart was still sitting down the fairway, now well over 100 yards away. It contained my putter, of course, and there was no alternative but to retrieve the cart while everyone in my group plus the group behind waited . . . and waited. Only then did they get to wait some more while I putted out.

After this comedy of errors I realized that there was a far better way. At some point after the carts are directed onto the path, you are in cart-path-only mode and will be for the remainder of the hole. Unless your ball is very near the path, any position inside this line is going to require you to walk back and forth to the cart at right angles to the line of play. This maneuvering has a point of diminishing returns. At some point it will actually involve less walking (and less time) to walk backward instead of sideways. For example, if your ball is in the middle of the fairway, it is likely 25 yards from the cart path. You will walk a total of 50 yards to hit just one shot. Why not deal with the business of parking the cart behind the green before hitting *any* shots, knowing that at least you will be able to play the remainder of the hole continuously? In such a case you will also obtain the benefit of observing your line from above the hole as you walk back to your ball.

My experience revealed another compelling argument. For the average player, shots near the green are more difficult and, it follows, more frequent. Finesse shots such as the flop, the blast, and the pitch and run have a high degree of difficulty. In short, anything can happen. All too frequently a golfer is in a quandary. After missing a shot, does he continue play, as I

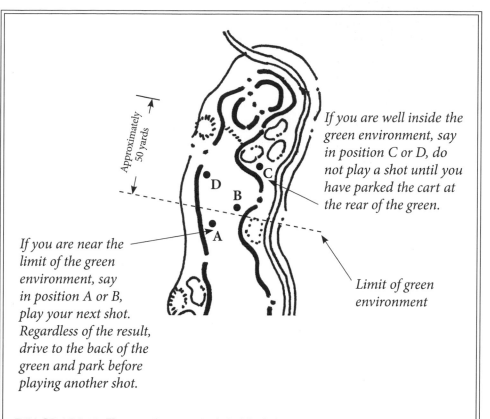

If you are well inside the green environment, say in position C or D, do not play a shot until you have parked the cart at the rear of the green.

If you are near the limit of the green environment, say in position A or B, play your next shot. Regardless of the result, drive to the back of the green and park before playing another shot.

Limit of green environment

Approximately 50 yards

DIAGRAM 10: *Know when to park behind the green and play the remainder of the hole on foot. The green environment starts when the carts are directed off the path, or about 50 yards from the green center, whichever occurs first.*

did, leaving the cart ever farther behind? Or does he return to the cart and reposition it? Usually the last thing on his mind is the cart. He essentially abandons it by walking after his ball and hitting it again. When his group finishes the hole, the cart is still there. He has committed the cardinal sin of cart management, leaving the cart in front of the green.

It is far better to get the cart parked and remove all chance of the above dilemma. Also better that the hole be completed without worrying about repositioning carts. If the game is to be enjoyed, play around the greens should be continuous and seamless. Because of this, *my foursome never hits greenside chips, pitches, or sand shots without first parking the carts behind the green.* (See Diagram 10.)

Positioning Carts at the Green

There are few things you can say with absolute certainty in golf, but this is one: There is only one correct place to park a cart at the green, and that is at the point where the path begins to leave the green environment for the next tee. Not where the path first approaches the green. Not where the path is alongside the center of the green. Not where the path is at the rear of the green. Not necessarily even where the path is behind the green.

Park the cart as far along the path as you can without actually departing the green environment.

Sometimes the path begins to peel away before it gets to the rear. In such cases, take the cart far enough to be well clear of the green. There are no degrees of correctness here. If the group behind can conceivably reach you with their shots, they must wait until you have stowed your clubs, gotten into the cart, and driven away. It is not good enough to park the carts green-high, or even toward the rear. The fact is that unless the path is an unusually long way from the green, they will have to wait unless you park the carts behind the green and leading away.

When the next hole is parallel and adjacent to the one you are playing, the cart path may make a 180-degree turn beyond the green to get to the next tee. If that tee is opposite and close to the green you are playing, and assuming it's unoccupied, it may make sense to take the cart all the way to the next tee box. Always seize any opportunity to avoid repositioning the cart, especially when it will involve only a short walk. (See Diagram 11.)

Bag Management

When golfers walk and carry their bag or pull a cart, the equipment goes where they go and there is nothing to manage. The only exception is at the green. *Here the advice for carts also goes for bags and pull carts: Don't leave them in front of the green.* Walkers often find themselves in the same dilemma as riders near the green. Let's say that your ball is 20 yards in front of a long, narrow green, with the pin near the back. You walk up to your ball, put your bag down, and execute the shot. But let's assume you hit it fat and your ball barely trickles onto the green. At this point do you carry your bag or walk your pull cart to the back of the green and backtrack all the way to the front to putt? Yes, absolutely.

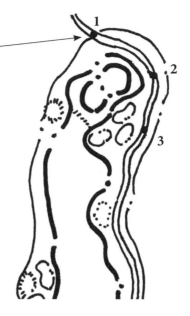

Once you have reached the green environment, the only place to park the cart is position 1. Do not park at position 2 or 3 or any other place.

DIAGRAM 11: *There is only one correct place to park carts at the green: where the path begins to depart the green environment for the next tee.*

Why? Because, as Woody Hayes said of the forward pass, three things can happen and two of them are bad. If you elect to putt with your bag on the front of the green, the only good thing that can happen is for you to sink the putt or have a gimmie, in which case your partner can toss your ball back to you, leaving you free to deal with your bag. Given the remote likelihood of this, the chances are excellent that one of the two following bad things will occur: Either you will hit a bad putt, in which case you could still be away, or you will hit a good putt, in which case you will probably be in someone's line or at least so close to their line or the hole to be annoying to them. In either event, action is required of you. You need to either putt again or mark your ball. Immediately you are in the position of breaking the continuity of play on the green in order to move your bag to the rear, or if you choose to leave your bag where it is and continue play, of causing those behind you to wait following completion of the hole while you walk to the bottom of the green to retrieve your bag.

Take bags or pull carts to a position off the green between the flagstick and the next tee before putting.

This can almost always be done without delay to your partners, as everyone in the foursome has things to do when arriving at the green. When you exit the green you can walk directly to the next tee without detouring to retrieve your equipment. On the other hand, if you have to retrieve your bag from the front of the green after completing the hole, *you will always, without exception, cause a delay.*

These bags have been left in front of the green. Players in the fairway must wait for them to be retrieved before they can hit.

SUMMARY: Always Take Carts and Bags to the Rear of the Green

- ♀ Move your cart to the rear of the green at the earliest possible moment. This will always be before playing any shots within 50 yards of the green unless your ball is right next to the cart path.

- ♀ When parking at the green, always park your cart as far along the cart path as possible without actually departing the green environment for the next tee.

- ♀ Don't hit greenside chips, pitches, sand shots, or putts before your cart is parked in its proper position at the rear of the green.

- ♀ If you are walking, put your bag or pull cart next to the green on a line between the flagstick and the next tee before putting.

CHAPTER 8

Do Your Housekeeping on Your Own Time

"If you could ban one thing from the course,
73 percent say slow players."
—*Golf* MAGAZINE POLL

GOLFERS PERFORM MYRIAD TASKS during every round that have little to do with ball striking—chores ranging from organizing clubs to cleaning cleats to keeping score. We have all witnessed these activities being performed at inappropriate times, such as when the player is supposed to be hitting a shot, or vacating the green so the group behind can hit.

We should all perform these housekeeping chores on our own time, when nothing else is expected of us.

Before Taking the First Tee

An efficient round begins before striking the first ball. You don't want to be rifling through your pockets or your bag during the round to find essential things. I begin each round with only these three things in my side pockets:

- Enough tees to play the round. Usually five or six will do.
- A visible ball mark, something about the size of a quarter. Anything smaller or darker can be hard to see, and if everyone can't see it, delays will result at some point.
- A green repair tool. A tee is not a substitute for a repair tool; tees take longer and do a bad job.

All you want in your side pockets when you play golf is a ball mark, some tees, and a green repair tool.

Before you tee off, personalize your balls with a magic marker so that they can be easily recognized. It's far easier to simply tell your partners who are helping you look for your lost ball that it has, say, "two red dots" than it is to try and remember the brand and number. And it's easier for you and them to spot and identify. Keep a marker in your golf bag; you'll be glad you did.

Sharing a Bag

When two players share the same set of clubs, delays are inevitable. It's obvious you cannot possibly be ready to hit a shot if another golfer is across the hole using the club you need. On the green, things get comical. It's only a matter of time before the players wind up on opposite sides of the green, 100 feet apart, with only one putter between them. It's also only a matter of time before both players arrive at the green empty-handed, each assuming the other has brought the putter. Sharing a bag is a major no-no.

Respect Your Playing Partners' Personal Space

A considerate player stands back and gives partners a little room when they are hitting their shots or putting, staying out of their back and through lines, and not moving around while they are hitting. Golf is hard enough without having to hit while someone in your vision is moving around. And it takes long enough without having players step back to start their routine over because someone didn't have the courtesy to be quiet and still during the fraction of a second it takes for someone else to strike the ball.

Cell Phones

It's tempting to say that cell phones should be banned from golf courses. But this will never happen because they are so pervasive and, frankly, too useful. But we can set some ground rules. First, ringers should be off. If not, it's only a matter of time before one goes off at the wrong time, which will cause golfers to step away as they are about to hit, or worse, as they are hitting, which will likely trigger demands for a do-over. Either way, time is wasted.

Second, a player on a phone call whose turn it is to hit should have two choices. Either he puts the phone down and hits straightaway with no pre-shot activity, or he signals to the rest of the group that he is withdrawing from, and forfeiting, the hole. Your foursome should agree to this policy before a round begins.

Checking emails and texts and answering them are silent activities which be done without disturbing anyone, and can be done during the considerable down time that occurs in every golf game. The arrival of these technologies has actually made it possible for busy people to disappear from their offices for four hours, yet stay connected. That's a good thing, since otherwise they likely wouldn't be able to play golf.

Replacing Divots

It is every golfer's obligation to replace divots. A solid divot can travel 10 yards or so. Be aware that if you are near one of your playing partners when making a shot, you can save the foursome a little time by tossing a divot back as you proceed up the fairway.

Time can be saved in another way. In certain instances it is actually counterproductive to replace a divot. When the divot isn't deep enough to remove a substantial amount of root material and soil, it won't survive, and replacing it will only inhibit restoration. This is a judgment call, and only through experience can we learn to recognize when a divot is too thin to replace. Also there are certain grasses, most notably Kikuyu and Bermuda, that aggressively regenerate by creeping horizontally. Bermuda or

Kikuyu divots rarely contain much soil because of their tangled structure, and should not be replaced.

Putting Clubs Away

Develop the habit of moving away before replacing your clubs after you have hit a shot or finished a hole. We've all seen players stand in the

These players have gotten into the cart immediately after hitting and will wait to put their clubs away until they have cleared the landing zone.

*To clear the landing zone immediately after hitting his shot,
this player is putting his clubs away as he walks up the fairway.*

middle of the fairway wiping down clubs, putting on head covers, even rearranging their clubs. This is torture to watch if you are waiting. If you are walking, hoist your bag on your shoulder and put your clubs into the bag as you walk. If you are riding, hold on to them until you get to the next tee or your partner's ball. You can easily drive a cart while holding onto a couple of clubs with your left hand.

Keeping Score

In a four-hour round of golf, there is plenty of time to keep the most elaborate scorecard one can envision, even considering multiple presses and complex betting schemes. In fact, there are only a few times when a scorekeeper won't be free to update his card. Every scorekeeper should wait for these times, when nothing else is expected of him.

Most golfers know not to stand on the green writing down scores while the group behind is waiting, but it is surprising how often you see players pausing just off the green to do it. This is a bit like the ostrich putting his head in the sand. Standing just off the green may seem less offensive but in fact it is no less; if the group behind has to wait, they have to wait. There is only one correct way to handle this. *All players should walk directly off the green at the conclusion of play, and the scorekeeper should not reach for the card until clear of the green environment.*

A player who does not have the honor is free to record scores. A player who does have the honor shouldn't deal with the scorecard *until after teeing off.* Then scores can be recorded at the player's leisure.

Eating at the Turn

Grabbing a drink or a sandwich to go at the turn is normal behavior if a group is keeping up. However, if a foursome is behind, the turn is a chance to catch up. The group should go directly to the 10th tee.

This is a no-brainer. Any group that is already behind and stops—actually comes to a halt, which is exactly what stopping at the turn is—is being doubly inconsiderate. Think of it as though you were in the ninth fairway, with people waiting, and stopped for five or 10 minutes to have a smoke and a beer; the effect is the same. Skipping a stop at the turn is the only opportunity we have to catch up without actually having to do anything golf-related. Every foursome that is behind should take advantage of this.

Bunker Play

It is basic to golf etiquette that a player will leave a bunker in the same or better condition than he found it. This takes time. It takes a lot more time if we have walked all over the bunker getting to our ball, or if we have to go searching for a rake after we hit the shot. There is a simple, but specific, procedure to follow when you have to hit a bunker shot:

Pick up a rake on the way to the bunker, and enter the bunker at the point closest to your ball, taking the rake with you.

It is far easier to walk around most bunkers than to rake a long line of footprints because of entering too soon. Similarly it is far easier to obtain a rake before the fact, because if not, you will need to retrace your steps twice to accomplish it after the fact, making even more footprints to rake. If the rake and point of entry are not in the same vicinity, it might be even more efficient to have a partner who is nearby toss you one.

A word of caution here. "Entering at the closest point" shouldn't always be taken literally. Some bunkers have very steep faces which could actually be dangerous to walk on. Also, walking on steep faces can cause some bunker edges to collapse, which certainly wouldn't qualify as leaving the bunker in better condition than you found it. Use common sense in deciding where to enter.

This player is entering a bunker near his ball and has a rake with him.

When you have finished raking the bunker, replace the rake in a logical place. This may not be where you found it or where you entered the bunker. It should be put in the bunker, near an edge, and well separated from any other rakes. If two rakes are right together, it means that another part of the bunker is missing one and that will eventually inconvenience someone.

In the special case of two players near each other in the same bunker, a little teamwork is in order. Only one rake is required. Both players should hit before any cleanup is done. The player hitting the best shot is rewarded with the task of raking up while the partner, who is away, goes off to hit again.

Rakes in Carts

I have played at courses where there are no rakes in the bunkers. Instead they are on the carts. I consider myself a pretty alert golfer, but reaching into the cart to obtain a rake is so counterintuitive that I (and most people I play with) can never remember to do it. The result is that either time is wasted or bunkers don't get raked. This innovation, if you can call it that, might possibly work if it became the policy at all courses and everyone got used to it. But this seems unlikely. For now this asks golfers to remember yet another thing in the campaign for fast play, and it isn't working.

Repairing Ball Marks

As we've said, golfers should *always* have a green repair tool in their pocket. Repairing a ball mark is as satisfying a task as there is in golf, as it usually means you have hit the green in regulation. You should repair your mark as a first order of business when arriving at the green. It should only take a moment, providing you can locate the mark. Finding your mark is yet another example of how you can save time by being alert. If you did not have a blind shot and you watched your ball in the air, you should have a pretty good sense of where it landed, even if it rolled a considerable distance after landing. For the ordinary player who typically doesn't spin the ball like the pros, the mark will usually be well before the final resting place of the ball. If you are walking onto the green, take a route that follows the line of your shot. Keep your head up and scan the surface so that you can locate the mark as soon as possible. If you are carrying your bag, you can

This player is repairing his ball mark as he crosses the green to place his bag at the rear. He can easily do this with his bag on his shoulder, killing two birds with one stone.

repair the mark on your way to placing your bag at the rear of the green, without even taking it off your shoulder.

SUMMARY: Do Your Housekeeping on Your Own Time

- Begin every round with only three things in your side pockets: tees, a ball mark, and a green repair tool.
- Stay well clear of the others in your foursome, and be quiet and still when they are hitting.
- Cell phone ringers should be off. If a call is important enough to take, the player should be prepared to forfeit the hole.
- Understand when divots should be replaced and when not. If nearby, toss a divot back to your partner after he hits.
- After hitting a fairway shot, walk or drive away toward the green before putting your clubs back into your bag.
- Always walk off the green and out of range of the group behind before reaching for your scorecard. If you have the honor on the next tee, hit before recording any scores.
- Do not stop at the turn for food if you are behind.
- If your ball is in a bunker, enter the bunker at the point closest to your ball, and have a rake with you.
- Always repair your ball marks, but not while others are waiting for you to putt.

CHAPTER 9

Know Yourself and Your Playing Partners

"If you pick up a golfer and hold it to your ear like a conch shell and listen, you will hear an alibi."
— P. G. WODEHOUSE

IF WE ARE REALLY CONCERNED about slow play we should look in the mirror and honestly assess our own performance. A poll taken by *Golf Digest* revealed that 58 percent of golfers called themselves fast players, and only 5 percent labeled themselves slow. The same golfers said that 56 percent of *other* players are slow, while only 2 percent are fast. In short, it's always the other guy's fault. Sigmund Freud would have agreed; this is the very definition of denial.

The first step toward addressing this is to admit, as an alcoholic should, that we have a problem. Beginners might realize that they play slowly, but experienced golfers don't like to admit that they've fallen into bad habits. Well, many of us have. It's painful to admit, but sometimes we're guilty of the behavior we complain about in others.

So it's time to take a close look at ourselves just to make sure we aren't part of the problem. Consider the following stereotypes.

The Absent-Minded Professor

We have all played with the guy who just doesn't seem to know what's going on. When he's away he will stand glassy-eyed behind his putt. You think he's studying his line and is about to walk up and hit it, but it turns out he's just daydreaming. He'll stand there forever if somebody doesn't remind him that he's actually on a golf course and everyone is waiting for him to hit. Alert and aware? This is the antithesis.

He doesn't know what to do with the cart. He loses clubs. He looks for lost balls 50 yards from where they flew into woods. You know the routine. What to do? He's not a bad person because he isn't even aware that he's being inconsiderate, so it's not a chewing out he needs. What he does need is a jolt back into the present. And you need to be persistent. The nature of the Absent-Minded Professor is that he is, well, absent-minded, so it's not likely that you can easily change his behavior. However, if you keep reminding him of his obligation to pay attention and you do it in a nonbullying way, he will respond and get the picture. "Yo, Bill, it's your turn to hit!" All you want is for the progress of the game to stay on his radar.

The Touring Pro

This person has watched *way* too much golf on TV. He's taking his role-model information from the touring professional. He sees and emulates all manner of mind-numbing behavior that is totally unacceptable on a public golf course. He's a rules stickler, so he hits provisional balls and searches endlessly for lost tee shots. He studies the yardage book before every shot. On any shot under 50 yards he ambles up to the green to view the contours. He crisscrosses the green studying his putt.

He marks his ball after every putt even if he is nowhere near anyone's line. And he putts *everything* out, even if it's for a quad.

I really don't need to describe this behavior because we've all seen it on TV. This is why it takes a threesome of professionals, with caddies and forecaddies, five hours to play a round. It should be obvious to all that this way of doing things just won't work on the local public course. You might want to say to this type of player, "Come on man, this isn't the U.S. Open!"

The Narcissist

The narcissist is all about himself. He may display some or all of the symptoms described below:

- He's looking really squared away in expensive and well-coordinated clothing. He's got all the best and newest gear. His bag, which may even have his name on it, is stocked with sleeves of new, top-of-the-line balls which, if not custom-printed with his initials, are neatly marked with his own very special concoction of color and design. If he pulls out a jacket or rain suit, you can bet it's the best money can buy. In short it's going to be really hard not to notice this guy.

- He exudes self-importance. He believes that his every shot will be viewed with compelling interest, and accordingly he will explain the details of his shots to anyone who will listen. "I caught that one a little thin. The lie was a little tight and I tried to pinch it but there was a small tuft of grass I was trying to avoid and I just missed the spot." Borrrriiiing! Meanwhile he completely ignores the play of others. His partner could make an eagle and he wouldn't even notice. But on the next hole he waits for the green to clear, even though he's 275 yards away.

- He's utterly oblivious to his shortcomings. He usually begins a round by saying something to set himself apart from the mediocre masses he is stuck with. (That's you.) He may announce that he will play from "the tips," remarking that "real" golfers (obviously implying that he is a charter member of that select community) always play from the back. When his initial drive slices into the woods, he tees up a provisional ball. Before hitting it he will likely say something like, "I haven't hit a shot that bad all year. I *never* slice the ball." When the next one slices and follows its sleevemate into the woods you might wonder if you have just witnessed some statistical anomaly—that is, until you realize that you've seen this guy this before, or at least someone just like him. He's not an Absent-Minded Professor, but still he doesn't know what's going on. That's because the Narcissist has a distorted view of reality. He fails to see himself in reasonable perspective to others and the world around him.

- Nothing is ever his fault. When his actual game falls short of his elevated sense of himself, which it always does, he is transformed into Alibi Ike of the well-loved Ring Lardner short story. He'll claim bad lie, unexpected noise, slippery grip, anything but a bad swing.

- When he plays *really* badly, look out. This outwardly proud, confident individual can slip into self-loathing. He will enter a self-absorbed funk, scowling, sulking, and noncommunicative. An outside observer would assume some horrible tragedy has befallen him, but all that's really happened is he's lost his swing, something that happens to us mortals all the time. He is, of course, unaware that this behavior places any burden on us.

As pointed out in the beginning of this book, a good check on yourself and others you might suspect of narcissistic behavior is simple: After completion of a hole does a golfer consistently know the score made by the others in the group? If not, then that golfer does not understand that he is part of a group—and that a successful round of golf is always the result of a group effort. Instead it's always about him. It's going to take years of therapy to change this guy, so don't even try. Don't make the mistake of indulging him by actually listening to his self-promoting and excuse-making, because he will feel reinforced and emboldened and he'll lay it on even thicker. I try to ignore these golfers. And I don't try to hide my disdain. If a guy wants to revisit his missed putt by hitting it again and again, I just put the flag in and say, "We gotta get moving. People are waiting," and walk away.

Mr. Do-Over

When Mr. Do-Over hits a rotten shot, he always wants to hit another. *Right away.* Before the ball has even come to rest he reaches into his pocket for a spare and is setting up to hit that one, too. What's he doing? It's not a mulligan he's hitting because the mulligan is a traditional second chance at a drive on the first tee and has no place elsewhere on the course. It's not practice. Practicing on the course is fine if you are alone or if the course is empty, but it can't possibly be done in a foursome on a busy day. It's not a provisional. His real ball is sitting 30 yards away in plain view, just where he topped it. What's he doing? He's being selfish and inconsiderate, that's what. Why doesn't it occur to him that we do not want to spend our Saturday afternoon watching him hit bad golf shots? Why doesn't it occur to him that after hitting two shots he has two balls to find and retrieve, and if we don't help him we only hurt ourselves because we'd otherwise have to wait while he does it?

Because he's angry and hurried, he usually hits the second one as badly as the first. Why can't he see what's obvious to everyone else—that he's actually developing careless habits and diminishing his game? Mr. Do-Over would benefit greatly from knowing that he will have to live with the consequences of his one and only shot, and therefore applying maximum concentration toward its outcome. His game would elevate, as would his character, not to mention the humor of his playing companions.

Once you are on to him, the remedy, as with the Narcissist, is to not indulge him. I pretend to be oblivious to his habit. I walk away and toward the hole after he has hit his original shot, and make it physically impossible for him to hit another—unless, that is, he is willing to drill me right in the back.

Obviously I feel pretty strongly about this. A mulligan on the first tee is okay, but whacking balls willy-nilly all over the course just isn't golf. It's up to you to decide what to do when you are alone on the course, but when others are waiting it crosses a line. Regardless of how discouraged we get with our play, *we should never hit do-overs while others—in our own group or the one behind—are waiting.*

Be a Leader

When we are playing with people whose behavior, whether they are aware of it or not, is ruining what may be our only chance to play that week, we don't have to sit idly by and suffer. We really can speak up, whether they are lifelong friends or people we just got paired with. And it's the right thing to do.

One savvy, alert player can do a lot to influence the behavior of a foursome. Resolve for that person to be you. Be a leader. If you are falling behind, you can point it out to your playing partners, even if they are strangers: "Hey, guys, we're falling behind and people are waiting on us. We really need to pick up the pace." They might not have noticed and will likely be grateful for the information. I say again, be a leader.

It's Alright to Complain ... Politely

The need to take the initiative will come up in another situation—when the group ahead is playing slowly, holding you up, with open space in front and no ranger in sight. If you are walking it can be difficult to make contact with them, but if you are in a cart you can easily race up and speak to them. You will have two choices in how to handle the matter. If there is no one behind you, you can politely say that while they might not have noticed, you have been waiting on them, and ask to play through. But if there are groups right behind you, playing through is not an option because it will only make things worse for those who follow. In this case you simply have to point out—politely, of course—that they are holding up play on the course and ask that they speed things up. Usually they will do just that, not wanting to be labeled as the pariahs who are blocking the whole course.

Some may find it difficult to confront strangers in this way. All I can suggest is that you try it. I think you will be surprised how easy and effective it is and, moreover, how relieved and liberated you will feel after you have done it.

Be Realistic about Your Ability

We shouldn't stand in the fairway waiting for the green to clear if it will require a career shot to reach the green. If there is one sure way to arouse anger in the golf gods it's to harbor delusions about one's ability to hit a demanding shot. In 99.9 percent of cases it will fall way short and we will feel pretty silly for waiting. Those on the tee behind will not be sympathetic. In the rare case when we do actually reach the green, the shot will retain all the power of a ping-pong ball as it trickles on and no harm will be done. The simple apology, "I had no idea I could hit it that far," will usually be well received. This is especially so on par-5s, as real golfers are always happy to see a fellow combatant reach the green in two.

Personally I would far rather see players hitting too soon than too late, even if it means occasionally having a ball trickle up on me. It's comforting to know that if I'm ever behind this person he won't be the one holding me up.

Establish an Efficient Routine

All good golfers have a set routine that they follow before every shot. Any teacher will tell you a routine is important for good, consistent play, but it's also important for fast play. This is because a given routine takes a given amount of time, and it stays consistent through the round. It leads to a reliable pace.

The catch is that some routines are agonizingly deliberate. They just take way too long. We have all suffered through a round with a player who, before every shot, stands behind the ball, takes two practice swings, then stands astride the ball, takes two more swings, moving all the while in slow motion before finally addressing the ball, then stands frozen for an

Establish an efficient routine. Ask a friend to time yours. Your routine should take no more than 20 seconds from the moment it is your turn to hit until you have actually struck the ball.

interminable time (presumably conducting a review of a lengthy catalog of swing keys) before actually taking a swing at the ball.

We all need to make sure that this does not describe our routine. We can have a friend time ours to make sure that the time from the moment it is our turn to hit until the moment we actually strike the ball does not exceed 20 seconds. This is not to make us feel rushed; it is to encourage us to develop a faster routine so that we do *not* feel rushed. As you will discover, 20 seconds is actually plenty of time. This may be a case, in the famous words of the architect Mies van der Rohe, of "Less is more." A longer routine isn't helpful, because standing static is not conducive to any athletic move. I'll bet you find that when you tighten up your routine you actually play better. For most people, *to play faster is to play better.*

SUMMARY: Know Yourself and Your Playing Partners

♀ Do an honest self-examination to make certain that you are not part of the problem.

♀ Learn to recognize those who are. Don't be afraid to speak up.

♀ Don't let others in your foursome ruin your day. Be a leader. Show them the way.

♀ It's permissible to politely complain to a slow group in front of you.

♀ Be aware of your own limitations so that you don't unnecessarily delay hitting your shots.

♀ Develop your own reliable preshot routine that takes less than 20 seconds from the moment it is your turn until you have struck your shot.

CHAPTER 10

Course Operations and Fast Play

*"Courses must be more playable
and less time consuming."*
—ARTHUR HILLS

IT'S PRETTY OBVIOUS THAT practically every decision golf course operators and greenskeepers make has an influence on pace of play. It is in the best interest of public courses to encourage a fast pace as this will translate into happier customers and more revenue. So it is something of a mystery that course operators haven't always done everything possible in this regard.

Tee Placement

Long, punishing courses are all the rage. But every course has to be playable for every customer, and distance is the first benchmark of playability. A golfer has no chance to play golf anything like it was meant to be played when two career shots are required to reach the par-4s, or when he can't reach the par-3s in one shot. It is the responsibility of the course to provide a set-up that avoids this for every class of player.

Many courses have only three tee boxes—championship (blue), men (white), and women (red)—and there isn't much flexibility to move up. However, most facilities could add two more colors without making any structural changes to the course at all. Five tee placements is ideal. They shouldn't be labeled as "men," "ladies," "seniors," and so forth, because no one wants to be stereotyped. Distance is all that should matter. In round numbers, tees at the following total distances should offer a home for everyone: 5,000 yards, 5,500 yards, 6,000 yards, 6,500 yards, and 7,000 yards.

Weather

Weather has a profound effect on course difficulty and pace of play.

- Cold temperatures reduce carry distance by about 2.5 percent for each 10-degree drop in temperature. Cold air is denser than warm air, and the resistance applied to a ball in flight increases as temperature drops, so that the ball doesn't carry as far. Pilots know this better than anyone, only in reverse. Pilots are wary of hot air; the biggest red flag in flying is "hot and high," which describes the conditions that make for very long takeoff runs in the reduced lift found in low-density air.

- Water evaporates slowly in cold air, so fairways stay damp, and roll is reduced or eliminated. A drive that rolls 40 yards is a totally different animal from one that plugs on impact. It's hard to predict the effect, but my experience has been that for every 10-degree drop in temperature, roll will be reduced by an average of another 2.5 percent. So between reduced carry and reduced roll, distance is cut by about 5 percent for every 10-degree drop in temperature. That 250-yard drive you hit at 70 degrees is reduced to 225 yards at 50 degrees. Another way of putting it: That 400-yard hole just became 440.

- As wind increases, the pressure it exerts is proportional to the square of its velocity. In other words, a 20-mile-per-hour wind knocks your ball down with *four times the force* of a 10-mile wind. When the wind pipes up over 25 miles per hour, the game is transformed. Winds like this can easily affect club selection by three or more clubs.

Course Setup and Weather

Given the previous discussion, it would seem logical that when cold or wind are expected, weather should become a primary factor in course setup. At most courses, setup is left to the greenskeeper, who is focused on course condition—moving tee markers and pins around to get even wear on the course. Greenskeepers aren't really too concerned about the customer experience—that's management's job. Courses that practice this division of responsibility could help their own cause with a little coordination because course set up and customer experience are totally intertwined, especially in bad weather.

It's inevitable that if greenskeepers don't pay attention to weather, some pretty absurd situations will arise: Tees all the way back facing directly into a gale. Howling downwind shots to pins right behind bunkers. Weather is part of the game, and so is adversity. But common sense should intercede at some point to keep the course playable and the pace reasonable.

Weather is predicted with great accuracy these days, and given that courses are set up each and every morning, it would seem a simple matter to make the day's decisions with the weather in mind. If it's hot and dry, stretch it out. But if there's a strong west wind and a west-facing hole requires driving the ball to the crest of a hill in order to see and reach the green, move the tees up. Common sense will improve the customer experience, keep balls in play, and quicken the pace of play.

Beverage Carts

Golfers need sustenance during four hours of combat, but this shouldn't contribute to the problem of slow play. Beverage cart operators should meet foursomes on a tee, where the whole group is certain to be together and where at least three of the golfers will be free at any given time. The golfers can work together, too, by having one of their group doing the buying for all four.

The worst place to meet is at a green, where there is a high likelihood that the group behind will have to wait. Meeting in the fairway isn't much better. But meeting behind a green is nearly as good as a tee. When a beverage cart stops at a green while the players behind are waiting, just ask the driver to meet you in a minute behind the green or up on the next tee.

Hazard and Yardage Markings

The better a course is marked, the faster it can be played. It's pretty obvious that play is delayed if people are wandering around trying to figure out whether they are in a hazard or not, or whether they are in a water hazard or a lateral hazard, and whether there is a drop area up ahead.

It's even more important to mark untended areas, even if on dry land, as hazards—places where it's unlikely that a ball can be found, such as tall grass, uncleared woods, and other areas that are not maintained. If a course decides to leave untended areas in play, it is inviting—virtually guaranteeing—provisional balls and lengthy search missions. The logical solution is to mark these areas as lateral hazards and give the rules-obsessed player a legal out. Huge amounts of time will be saved, and everyone—the player, the rest of the foursome, the groups behind, and the course operator—will be happier.

It's just as important to have a course well marked for yardage. The days of intuiting one's yardage went out with Young Tom Morris. Today's golfers want and deserve to know distances. It isn't enough to know how far away the green is, or even the pin. Depending on the situation it might be essential to know the distance to cross bunkers and hazards. I find it particularly galling to see sprinkler heads marked "Don't Even Think about It," or "In Your Dreams." Some might find this amusing, but just because you can't reach the green doesn't mean you aren't interested in where to lay up.

Golfers spend time deducing yardages to things, that's a given, and time is saved by better markings.

The advent of GPS monitors in carts is a positive innovation, albeit with the limitation that the cart must be able to drive right up to a golfer's ball to be effective. (It's not of much use when carts are confined to the paths or when a ball is in the woods or other terrain that is off limits to carts.) Nevertheless any course that has GPS in the carts has given its clientele a major tool to play faster.

Rakes

Bunkers without an adequate number of rakes are an invitation to golfers to spend time looking for and retrieving them or, alternately, not raking the bunkers at all. Both outcomes are bad, and both adversely affect pace of play.

Tee-Time Intervals

Golf courses generally send groups off at intervals ranging from seven to 10 minutes. Now theoretically, and I emphasize "theoretically," it should be possible to send groups off at eight-minute intervals. This is because in a four-hour round of golf, the average par-4 should take about 14 minutes to play. Accordingly, six or so minutes after teeing off

This bunker has three rakes, evenly spaced. After playing a bunker shot, the player should leave the rake about equidistant from the others.

on a par-4, a group should be hitting its second shots and the fairway should soon be open for the next group, and likewise the next, and so on through the day.

For this to work, however, will require perfect execution by each and every foursome. We all know that perfection is not possible, but even if it were, there will still be backups at the greens because more than half the allotted time is spent in the green environments. There will also be backups at the par-3s. This is because it takes about nine minutes to play the average par-3. And if backups are inevitable, every further glitch will make them worse. Presumably nobody in their right mind would design a system that, even if working perfectly, would cause backups, but if a course uses intervals of seven, eight, or even nine minutes, backups will be inevitable.

Compressing tee times ostensibly leads to more income for the daily-fee courses and helps the munis realize their goal of serving the maximum number of people. *This thinking is illusory.* It's like putting too many cars on a freeway; you can merge them in, but they will be immediately slowed because the facility can't accommodate them. An analogy can be made between tee times and the metering devices used on some freeway on-ramps, the purpose of which is to allow cars in at a rate that can be accommodated by the highway. If you use eight-minute tee times, after an hour one or two extra foursomes will have been force-fed onto the course, meaning a delay of 10 to 15 minutes imposed on all who follow. After two hours, another 10 or 15 minutes is added, and so on. By mid-morning the course will have almost certainly established a five-hour pace.

The munis aren't really serving more golfers, and the daily-fees aren't really making more money. This is because golfers won't make tee times within five and a half hours of sunset. Because of the slow pace, courses will lose many potential afternoon foursomes to darkness.

Any interval less than nine minutes will virtually ensure a slow pace. Given that, at best, a nine minute interval will barely work, complex or difficult courses are well advised to set 10-minute tee times.

Rangers

The main human interface between a course and its clientele is its crew of rangers. Sure, a player comes face to face with a teenager who takes clubs at the bag drop, the pro in the shop who takes the green fees, a starter, maybe a beverage person on the course, and possibly a bartender or server in the clubhouse. All are important, but all are peripheral to the actual business of playing golf. A ranger is the only employee who will monitor and assist a player on the course, and whether a golfer has a good experience or a bad one is largely in the ranger's hands. Accordingly rangers are, or should be, key employees at any thoughtfully operated course. If a course is to establish a culture of fast play, *it will not happen without a crew of effective rangers.*

We have all interacted with rangers at times. They are usually retirees working mostly for playing privileges. They love golf, yes, but it's no more certain that a golf lover will own the unique skills to be a ranger than it is certain he will have a 2 handicap. The job requires the wisdom of Job and the tact of a diplomat. A good ranger needs to be knowledgeable, like-able, and patient, yet unmistakably firm—a "people person" with a unique social antenna. After all, the job is to chastise paying customers without alienating them. Not an easy task. It's time to elevate this job to a place of importance, with training and decent pay, because it is without question as challenging a job as one will find in the golf business. Only people with a suitable temperament and personality need apply.

The first thing the ranger must understand is what constitutes an appro-priate pace. Many courses have decided that they are four-and-a-half-hour courses. By doing this, they have already lost the battle. It's human nature that if you set a goal that's too low, you are doomed to mediocrity and you will automatically perpetuate the problem you are trying to solve. It will also ensure that anyone who has learned to play at a proper pace will have a bad experience. The course will, in effect, alienate its best clients. There is only one proper pace. *Under four hours is the proper pace.*

We've discussed at length what this means to the golfer—20 seconds to hit each shot, parking behind the green, and so on. To the ranger it means something a little different. It means approximately 14 minutes to play a par-4, nine minutes to play a par-3, and 17 minutes to play a par-5. A little more than half this time is spent in the green environment. These approximate times are averages and cannot be applied blindly to every hole. A wide-open 130-yard par-3 will take less time to play than a 220-yard monster over water. So a pace guide needs to be customized for each course, assigning a time to play each hole that may be somewhat above or below the average based on relative difficulty, but still totaling less than four hours. Once this guide is established for a given course it will predict the elapsed time it should take to arrive at a given place on the course, and this information, coupled with a group's starting time, will allow a ranger to tell at any point whether a given group is on pace.

A lot of courses already do this in one form or another, but without using it properly it doesn't make much difference. What good does it do, for example, to know that you are falling behind the pace when the course is jammed in front of you and you can't do anything about it?

The pace guide must be used, not just to monitor a group's progress, but *to prevent that group from falling behind in the first place.*

A ranger needs to understand *the unrelenting tyranny of accumulated gaps.* Consider this: If a group falls one hole behind—that's about 14 minutes—then every group for the rest of the day will likely be 14 minutes behind, because experience has told us that, once established, gaps are pretty difficult to close. After all, the group that caused the gap has already demonstrated it can't keep a normal pace; to close the gap will require them not just to meet that normal pace *but exceed it by a wide margin.* This is not likely without a draconian solution such as requiring them to skip an entire hole. Add a couple more 14-minute gaps, and you have a disaster on your hands. As the day wears on, the players causing these gaps may be finished and gone, but structural delays will have been established. At this point, information about a given group's pace is useless. Every group will be right on the tail of every other on their way to a five-and-a-half-hour round. The horse has left the barn, and it isn't coming back.

You have one chance and only one to control the pace of play, and that is at the beginning of the day. *The only way to achieve this—the only way—is not to allow gaps to begin in the first place.* This is the ranger's most important job: being on the course at the beginning of the day, before the first group tees off.

Later when the initial group hits the back nine, you will need a second ranger, one for each nine. One ranger cannot possibly monitor 200 acres of golf holes. And they need to communicate regularly about problem groups and bottlenecks.

Assuming a full tee sheet, the first groups out in the morning are key. These pacesetters will establish the tone for the day. If they don't, all is lost, because the system is only as strong as its weakest link. If they play faster than the established pace, that's fine. The ranger only needs to consult the guide and be sure not to chastise a following group that has fallen behind if, in fact, the following group is on the required four-hour pace.

If it's not a full tee sheet, things get tricky. Let's say the first group has two open tee times behind them before the course gets busy. If they get off to a slow start, no one is immediately affected, and it could be argued that no harm is done—until later groups catch up, that is. At that point you have a problem. The offending group has gotten used to its dawdling pace, and history has shown that behavior modification at that point is not easy. Instead, using the pace guide, the ranger needs to keep that group on pace from the beginning—from the very first hole, telling them that they will soon be hearing footsteps and that they need to keep the pace in order to stay out in front.

The starter and ranger can work together on this. The starter has to emphasize the heavy responsibility placed on the shoulders of *all the early groups—at least the first two hours' worth—to set the pace for the day.* Even if there are gaps in the early portion of the tee sheet, the starter should explain the destructive nature of slow play early in the day, inform the early foursomes of the required pace, and endow them with the responsibility to set it. Starters should tell these groups of their important role in the day's events for hundreds of people, and how everyone on the course is relying on them. Give them a goal. *Empower them.*

A tasteful, explanatory sign before the first tee will help. It could be titled, "We Are a Four-Hour Facility" and give further information about policies and how they will be enforced. Another sign at the conclusion of the first hole will serve as a reminder. Another at the conclusion of the 10th will keep the message current.

Also, rangers' carts should fly red flags that make it obvious to all when rangers are on the scene. Just seeing a ranger on a regular basis will help the pace of play. It keeps the issue on the front burner, and it reminds players that management is serious about a fast-play policy.

It Can Be Done

If a course has good rangering, at some point it will take on the reputation and culture of a fast-play facility, and things will become much easier. The example of Farm Neck Golf Course on Martha's Vineyard, Massachusetts, is instructive. This is a lovely resort course that plays along the salt ponds and wetlands of the island and enjoys stunning views of Nantucket Sound and beyond. It has several strikes against it in the battle for fast play because many who play it are visitors. They are on vacation and not in a hurry to do anything, they don't know the layout, and dazzled by the scenic beauty, they are forever pausing to take in the vistas. To make matters worse, it is a tight course interlaced with beautiful, but ball-grabbing, stands of pines.

Historically, playing Farm Neck was a long, slow slog. But about ten years ago management decided to do something about it. Areas behind holes 1 and 10, and all carts, were fitted with tasteful signage that announced that Farm Neck was a four-hour course and that the policy would be enforced. It's easy to announce something. Enforcement is the tricky part, given that in every instance the culprit would be a paying customer. The enforcers were, of course, going to be rangers.

Finding the right person to be a ranger is not an easy thing. At most courses, rangers are hired without much vetting and no training. Farm Neck took the opposite attitude, recognizing that rangers were the key to making the policy work, and thus were some of the most important hires the course would make. Management also recognized the importance of continuity and consistency in its rangering program and sought employees who would be with the course, not for just a season, but on a long-term basis.

It didn't happen overnight, but a few years after putting the policy into place the four-hour round was a reality. It has been ever since, even though it requires constant vigilance to keep it that way. The head ranger has been at Farm Neck for close to ten years, and now runs a program that trains the assistants not only in the logistics of fast play but in how to recognize the right approach to various individuals and situations. The course now has a reputation for fast play.

Special Policies

There are certain ideas that can be used to separate fast golfers from slow ones. Courses can conduct early morning shotguns for self-described fast players. These would be advertised as events only for sub-four-hour players. Camaraderie and enthusiasm could well develop around such a concept.

Another idea is to limit prime, early morning, tee times to better players with handicaps of perhaps fifteen or better on the theory that they will not play faster and be more compatible.

The problem with ideas like this is that they discriminate – they separate players with different abilities when one of the truly beautiful things about golf's handicap system is that it allows players of all abilities and ages to play together and actually compete against one another. For this reason the *best solution by far is to teach all players to play at a four-hour pace.*

What a Fast Play Program Looks Like

A course that has been able to develop a successful culture of fast play likely does the following things:

- **Media**. It makes clear at every turn that it is a *Fast Play Facility*. Every piece of written material on the course, whether advertising, flyers, yardage books, press releases, score cards, or web sites emphasizes that golf can and will be played at the course in four hours.
- **Staff Interaction**. When purchasing green fees and when greeted by the starter, every player is reminded that the course is a fast play facility and that they are expected to do their part. They are told that rangers will assist them as necessary to keep the pace, and help them understand how to do it.
- **Rangers**. It has a staff of trained rangers that it treats as valued employees with a key role in course operations.
- **Signage**. Tasteful signage in the carts and at the first and tenth tees reminds everyone of the policy. Another at the conclusion of the first hole serves as a reminder. One at the conclusion of the 10th keeps the message current. Other signs in key places remind of specific actions required, such as, "Take carts to the rear of the green," or "Please do not stop after nine holes if you are behind."

In short, the course sends its message at every opportunity and helps players achieve their goals. Once this has taken hold, its reputation will spread through the golfing community. It will be known and revered for what it has accomplished.

SUMMARY: Course Operations and Fast Play

- ♀ Create maximum flexibility in distance by having five tee placements ranging in total distance from about 5,000 yards to about 7,000 yards.
- ♀ Be especially cognizant of bad weather when selecting tee and pin placements for the day.
- ♀ Develop a ranger training program at your course. Give this the highest priority.

- Train beverage cart operators to engage golfers behind greens and on tees only.
- Make sure your course is well marked, that it allows pull carts in the green environment, and that bunkers are well supplied with rakes. Add GPS to carts.
- Set intervals in tee times at nine or ten minutes depending on the difficulty of the course. Anything less than nine minutes will almost guarantee a slow pace.
- Develop a comprehensive media and staff training program to get the message out: You are a *Fast Play Facility*.

CHAPTER 11

Change the Culture

"I have no idea why anyone would want to hit two woods and a wedge on every hole. What's the fun in that?"
—ALICE DYE

ALICE DYE WAS REFERRING, of course, to the almost obsessive habit many golfers have of playing from distances that are incompatible with their ability. This seems to be ingrained in the golfing mind-set nowadays, and it is but one example of the many ways we have created a culture of slow play. We need to change this; the goal is to create a culture of fast play.

Those of you who are past middle age will remember a time when we didn't wear seat belts (when, in fact, cars didn't even have them), when nearly everybody smoked, when we routinely got in our car and drove home after a night of drinking. These things have been buried in the past. Nowadays we always wear seat belts. Many fewer people smoke (it isn't even allowed in most public spaces). And most wouldn't think of driving after a night of partying.

Clearly it's possible to enact change, even of longstanding and deeply ingrained practices such as these. The change required in golf is child's play by comparison. So, clearly, it can be done. It just needs to be moved to the front burner. Collectively, we in the golfing community can defeat the demon of slow play and change the culture of our game.

Golf in Britain

Recently I was with one of my sons at a local daily-fee course. As we all know, when you are a twosome at a busy course, it isn't fun to play alone because you will be trapped between foursomes and no matter what the pace it will seem like a long day. On the other hand, when you are paired with strangers there is always the risk that you will wind up with people whom, well, you wouldn't choose to play with again. But it's also an opportunity: You might meet people you really enjoy playing with, making for a great experience. It's a little like a long shot over water; it's a risk-and-reward thing.

On this occasion we were paired with Pat and Warren, an obvious mother-son duo who looked to be more or less age matched with my son and me. They were English as it turned out. Warren was working in the United States, and his mother was visiting. They had been playing golf together practically his whole life. It turned out to be a serendipitous pairing. We shared similar attitudes about all things golf—similar levels of devotion, similar abilities, similar histories. We had played many of the same courses in the British Isles. We were all four true aficionados.

It was a slow day on the course, and much of the conversation during that otherwise pleasant afternoon was on the subject of fast play. Warren and Pat held that in the British Isles a child learns from the first day holding a club that *keeping up is the most important part of golf etiquette.*

Golf in Britain is nearly as common as baseball in America. There are neighborhood courses everywhere, and almost anyone can play. I suspect that the availability of golf, and hence the opportunity to introduce it widely at a young age, parent to child, together with its long, long history has a lot to do with this culture. All golfers need to think more like the Brits.

Tee It Forward

Long courses are here to stay. But let's face it, most of us are playing them from the wrong tees. Guys like to be macho, probably because we identify too closely with the pros on TV. But we are shooting ourselves in the foot if we can't reach the par fours in two, or the par threes in one. Barney Adams, founder of the clubmaker Adams Golf, recently conducted an interesting experiment with professional-level players. Pros average about 285 yards off the tee, and after comparing this with the performance of mere mortals, he determined that for a pro to experience golf in the same way the average golfer experiences it, the pro would be playing an 8,000-yard course. So he put them back there on temporary tees and played golf with them. After needing a wood to reach most of the par-4s, the exasperated pros declared that they weren't having any fun and that it didn't seem fair. Barney replied, "Welcome to our world!"

We don't need to put good players at 8,000 yards. We can easily level the playing field by simply *moving up a tee or even two*. This is what the "Tee it Forward" movement is all about. If you can't hit a drive more than 200 yards, you shouldn't be playing a 400-yard par-4, or for that matter one that's shorter but, for reasons of grade or weather, *plays* 400 yards. The same goes for a guy who hits it 240 playing a 480-yard par-4. That's just common sense. This act alone would speed play considerably, and golf would be a lot more fun for most players.

Many in the know have spoken on this subject. One general manager said simply, "More men should be playing from the red tees." A noted golf writer said, "Too much testosterone is the problem!"

Each of us needs to find the distance that is right for us, whether it be 5,000 yards, 5,500 yards, 6,000 yards, 6,500 yards, or 7,000 yards. And we need to be realistic. The right distance is the one that lets us play the game as it was meant to be played, by which I mean that if we hit decent shots (not career shots, just decent ones for our level of play) we can reach the greens in regulation.

The next time you play, pay attention to this guideline. If after a decent drive on a tough hole you need a long iron for your approach, or on a shortish hole, a short iron or wedge, you are where you should be. If on the other hand (and this is what we see all too often) you are forever pulling out your three wood, you need to move up. You will enjoy the game a lot more, and so will you playing partners.

Weather

As we saw in the last chapter, cold temperatures and wet conditions play havoc with golf shots, reducing carry distance and roll to an extent that most of us would never imagine. A good rule of thumb is that on a wet, fifty-degree day we can subtract ten percent from our fair weather shots. Do the math. On a 400-yard hole it effectively adds forty yards, which translates to adding *four clubs* on an approach shot. Instead of a 7-iron we'll need to use a three! Wake up! This is a serious difference.

Wind is also a wicked foe on the course due to the empirical relationship between velocity and pressure. A 20-mile-per-hour wind knocks your ball down with *four times the force* of a 10-mile wind. This can affect approach shots by several clubs.

One would hope and assume that course operators would understand the effects of cold and would move up the tees during rotten weather. But if they don't, we can take matters into our own hands. When it's cold, we can feature our brain cells instead of our testosterone and play up a tee.

Let's say our foursome normally likes to play at about 6,500 yards. When we are out on a cold, damp, and blustery day we might look for tees at 6,000 yards. And we shouldn't feel at all unmanly, because even at 6,000 yards the course is going to play longer than the 6,500 we normally like to play.

One would also hope and assume that course operators would factor wind into setup. But if not, an easy fix in unusually strong winds is to play different holes from different tees depending on whether they are upwind or downwind. I say in unusually strong winds. The point is not to eliminate the challenges of wind but simply to make a course playable when, due to setup, it otherwise would not be.

GPS and Lasers

The thoughtful golfer will spend time deducing yardages to things, and a lot of that time can be saved with hand-held GPS and laser devices.

The hand-held GPS is a versatile tool because it works anywhere on the course. But it is imperfect because it cannot recognize pin placement, leaving the golfer to deduce (from flag color or a daily pin sheet) the actual distance to a given flag.

In many ways the best technology has to offer is found in the hand-held laser. This device gives precise distances to anything, whether it be a pin, a bunker, a tree, or even the group in front, should we be doubtful about whether they are too close for us to hit. It delivers the information on demand, easily, accurately and immediately. It's like having a genius caddy in your back pocket.

We should avail ourselves of everything technology has to offer. And what we all hope for is the ultimate timer saver: a golf ball that can be individually recognized by some kind of hand-held device. This would bring an end to searching for lost balls and as such would enormously elevate enjoyment of the game. The world will beat a path to the door of the inventor of such a device, and golfers everywhere will treat him like a god.

Tee-Time Intervals

The previous chapter contained a discussion of the merits of various tee time intervals. Before you book a tee time, you might think of asking the course what its tee time interval is. On a crowded day you can take any interval of less than nine minutes to mean you will be in for a long slog.

Adopt Some Ground Rules

If you have a regular group you play with, you might think of adopting some do's and don'ts that you can all agree on—things that will be constant every time you play. Some or all of the following would be good candidates, arranged more or less in descending order of importance:

Don't
- Hit provisional balls.
- Hit do-overs.
- Use a stroke-play format.
- Stop at the turn if your group is behind.
- Penalize for balls lost under autumn leaves.
- Engage a beverage cart in a location where other groups must wait.
- Mark your ball unless it is in or close to the line of another player's ball.

Do
- Play lost balls and shots out-of-bounds as lateral hazards.
- Live with your first and only shot.
- Pick up after you've hit the maximum for your handicap—or eight shots at most.
- Use a match-play format.
- Move up a tee in cold weather.
- Putt long putts with the flag in if no one is available to tend.
- Mark your playing partners' balls on the greens if it will save time.
- Rake the area before hitting if your ball is in a footprint in a bunker.
- Turn off cell phone ringers.

Practice Good Habits

There will be many times when we play on an uncrowded course and it isn't really necessary to play at any particular pace. We should guard against using such occasions to fall into bad habits. Fast play should become fully incorporated into the way we conduct ourselves on the course, not something that we turn off and on. After all, playing fast isn't something we learn just to placate the people playing behind. It's as much to increase the pleasure of the game for ourselves and our companions. Fast play should become second nature and a way of life on the course.

Take These Lessons to the Course

After reading this book it may appear that playing faster involves a grueling and obsessive commitment to a lot of minutiae, and that the game won't or can't be any fun under this kind of pressure. This is wrongheaded. Instead it should be viewed as behavior that will actually *relieve* the pressure we all feel when we know we are holding others up, behavior that will *ease* the frustration of slow play.

Sure, it will take some doing to become faster players. But it's nothing like the effort required to become better golfers—much faster to learn, much easier to ingrain, and unlike the golf swing, it won't desert you when you least expect it. Learn it once, and it's with you for life.

It goes without saying that you won't possibly be able to recall everything in the book when you play your next round. But I think you will be surprised how quickly things come into focus if you are committed to playing faster.

- First and foremost, be a zealot about situational awareness. Keep your head up and take in the details. *Notice things and act on them.*
- Second, remember that *delays are built in tiny increments.* Keep your eyes on the prize. Recognize small misdemeanors and act to correct them right away.
- Third, *be a team player and a leader.* Take the initiative to help your partners in the myriad ways we have discussed. They will learn by your example, and your efforts will be returned manyfold.

Don't be part of the problem; be part of the solution. And when you run into golfers who are part of the problem, you might let them know that this book is likely available at the pro shop for purchase when the round is over.

SUMMARY: Change the Culture

- Move up a tee or two if you can't reach most par-4s with a mid-iron on your second shot. If there isn't enough flexibility in tee placement, ask your course to add more.
- Play fast as a matter of habit, not just when the course is crowded.
- Be especially cognizant of bad weather when selecting your tees for the day.
- Inquire about the intervals in tee times when you decide where to play. Take anything less than nine minutes to mean you could be in for a long day.
- Develop situational awareness and a cooperative team attitude, and remember that delays are always built in tiny increments.
- Adopt permanent time-saving ground rules to use when you are playing with your regular partners.

AFTERWORD

"Golf is not a funeral, but both can be sad affairs."
— BERNARD DARWIN

IT'S NOT LIKELY THAT the golf writer Bernard Darwin was referring to slow play. But if he were alive today he probably would be.

Despite all the complaining about slow play, it persists. It certainly isn't getting better with a new generation of players taking up the game in lockstep with the worldwide surge in daily-fee course construction. The governing bodies of golf, the golf press, and the owners and operators of golf courses all bemoan the fact that the game takes so long to play, but the problem doesn't get any better. The silence on this subject is, as the saying goes, deafening.

One thing is for sure: It's not the fault of the new public golfers. They fell in love with the game. They pay their green fees. It's not their fault that nobody has shown them what to do. They didn't grow up playing the game, on club courses, supervised by parents and instructors. They missed out on a lot. So much is learned by osmosis when you are young, impressionable, and anxious to learn. That's a big vacuum to fill. No, it's not their fault. It's a failure of the stewards of the game that they haven't recognized and dealt with the emerging problem of slow play.

Is it a pipe dream to think that every golfer—young and old, beginner and expert, man and woman—can play in four hours?

It's been proven in the real-life laboratory of countless foursomes in all quarters who have figured out, on their own, how to play fast without hurrying. Those who cared about the game and wanted a better experience paid attention to what was happening in their group and those around them and figured it out. They did it by trial and error.

My regular foursome usually finishes a round in under four hours if we aren't held up by those in front. Sometimes we ride in carts, and sometimes we walk. If we're playing a new course, it might take a little longer; if we're on our home course, we might complete the round in a little less. We don't attempt to beat the clock or to set any particular pace. The regular members of the group—the foursome plus the frequent alternates—have handicaps between 10 and 27, and most of us are well into, or past, middle age. Most of us are experienced, but none are exceptional golfers. Under four hours is our normal pace.

I repeat: *Under four hours is our normal pace.* It is not fast, and we do not feel rushed. As I said, we are not exceptional golfers in any way. If we can figure it out while flying blind, then anyone can. So, no, I don't think it's a pipe dream that all golfers can play fast.

I keep coming back to young Rory McIlroy, as he seems to represent all that is good and hopeful about the dilemma of slow play. Sure, he is a much better player than any of us. But the way he goes about his business doesn't really have anything to do with ball striking. It's about attitude. It is obvious that for him the pleasure of golf is partly found in playing the game in the right way—observing proper etiquette, caring for the course and its occupants, and playing at a reasonable pace.

There's a big reward out there if we can collectively make this happen. That reward is to know that when we leave our house in the morning to play golf we can reliably predict the hour that we will return. It is to know that the pleasure of golf will depend, not on the behavior of people we will never meet, but only on the state of our game and the humor of our companions. In short it is to know that we can play the game as it was meant to be played.

Sam Dunn
February 2013

Signature Keys to Fast Play

Before You Play

- Develop a pre-shot routine that takes no more than twenty seconds from the moment it is your turn to hit until you actually strike the ball.
- Have only these things in your side pocket before you tee off: A ball marker, a green repair tool and several tees.
- Personalize your balls with a magic marker so they can be quickly recognized.
- Turn off cell phone ringers.
- Select the tees you play based on your realistic ability. If you can't reach most holes in regulation move up a tee. Keep the weather in mind. Move up another tee on blustery, cold days.

Maintaining a Fast Pace

- Keeping pace means your foursome should be ready to hit from the tee or in the fairway as soon as the group in front has vacated the landing area. And it means walking off the green before the group behind is ready to hit.
- You have only twenty seconds to hit each shot. If you are a beginning player, you are going to have to hustle because it is likely that you will be hitting more than one shot each time it is your turn. *Find it and hit it!*
- The most important thing you can do to facilitate this is to be ready to hit when it is your turn. Don't wait until your turn comes up to select a club or read your putt. Get ready at the earliest possible moment.

- Always know who has the honor. If it is you, take the tee and hit straightaway.
- Don't ever hit do-overs on a crowded course.
- Don't adhere obsessively to the concept of "away." There will be many occasions when hitting out of sequence will be necessary to keep up. Play "Ready Golf" if others aren't hitting when they're supposed to.
- Enter bunkers close to your ball and carry a rake with you.
- When on the green the player closest to the hole becomes the "conductor," announcing who is away, tending the flag, knocking balls away when putts are given, and marking them when they are not.
- There is no need to mark your ball unless it is in someone's line.
- Pick up after the maximum under your handicap range. If you don't have a handicap pick up after eight shots or less.
- Don't stop at the turn if your group is behind.

Rules of Golf

- In recreational play you can use the concept of the "last known point" in the flight of the ball as if it were the margin of a hazard. Drop at that point with a one-stroke penalty. This will eliminate hitting provisional balls in the case of shots potentially hit out-of-bounds or lost.
- Putt without removing the flagstick if you are a long way from the hole and no one is available to tend the flag.
- When a ball is missing but known to be in an area of fallen leaves, take a free drop and move on.
- Take a free drop in a bunker when your ball is in a footprint.

Lost Balls

- When your shot is in flight and headed off the fairway, watch it intently. Note a landmark in the vicinity of where it disappears into woods or untended areas.
- Watch the shots of your playing partners, not just your own.
- Listen intently for the sound of impact of errant shots to obtain a clue of their whereabouts.
- Look for lost balls in a rectangular area centered on a landmark. The rectangle should be longer than it is wide because direction is easier to assess than distance.

- Help companions look for lost balls unless yours is lost, too.
- If people behind are waiting stop looking about a minute after it is your turn to hit. Drop one and move on.
- If you are driving and playing with walkers, use the cart to locate their balls while they are walking up the fairway.

Cart Management

- Try to ensure that both occupants of a cart are doing something to advance the round at every possible moment. Be aware that both will need to drive the cart at various times.
- The player with the shortest drive should be dropped off at his ball. The other player should then drive to his ball as long as it is not in he line of the first player's shot. After hitting, the first player should start walking up the fairway to join the cart. This process should be repeated as you advance along the hole.
- Never leave the cart without having every conceivable club you may need to execute your next shot. This also applies to greenside situations when your ball is not actually on the green.
- When you return to the cart after hitting your approach shot get into the cart holding your clubs and drive to your next shot before putting them away.
- When carts are confined to the paths take clubs you need to hit your next shot and one after that too, in case you hit a bad one If you are a really long way from the path consider taking your whole bag and finishing the hole on foot.
- If you and your cart-mate are near your opponent's cart and they are both on the other side of the hole, one of you can drive it up to the green for them.
- If your approach shot misses the green on the opposite side of the hole from the cart path, you might as well let your partner handle the cart while you take a few clubs and plan to finish the hole without returning to the cart.
- If you are dropped off within about 50 yards of the green take everything you will need to finish the hole—usually a couple of wedges and a putter—and finish on foot.

- If you are driving and your ball is inside the point where carts are directed off the fairway take the cart to the rear of the green and walk back to your ball before hitting.
- Always park carts behind the green so that when you walk off the group behind can hit right away.
- Before putting place your extra clubs on the green in a line between the hole and the cart so you will be sure to notice them as you exit the green.

Leadership and Demeanor

- Be alert and aware!
- Playing fast takes a team effort. Watch your partners' shots. Help them by bringing them a club, giving a distance, driving their cart.
- Stay aware of the position of your group with respect to those ahead and behind.
- Be the one to prod your foursome into faster play if you are falling behind.
- Do not be shy about confronting a slow group in front of you, or about complaining to a ranger.
- Be a leader!

ACKNOWLEDGMENTS

Thanks to Fran Day, Pete Lustig, and Steve Goodwin, the long-suffering members of my regular foursome who, with mostly good cheer, served as guinea pigs for the fast-play strategies in the book.

Tim Sweet and Glen Field of Farm Neck Golf Course in Massachusetts for showing me the importance of rangers.

Ted Goodenow and the staff at Whiskey Creek Golf Course in Maryland for walking me through the operation of a daily-fee course.

My wife, Eleanor, and children, Josh, Sammy, and Ollie, for reading the book—in Eleanor's case, several times—and making many helpful suggestions.

Finally my good friend Steve Goodwin—professor of creative writing, novelist, golf design critic, and distinguished golf writer of many decades standing—for helping every step of the way. He's a true believer when it comes to golf.